INTRODUCTION

Welcome to the "Ninja Dual Zone Air Fryer CookBo
We are thrilled to have you embark on this culinary journey with us.

Cooking is not just a mere act of nourishment; it is an art that evokes emotions and creates memorable experiences. We understand the joy and satisfaction that comes from preparing delicious meals for yourself and your loved ones. That is why we have poured our hearts into curating this cookbook, with the aim of igniting your culinary creativity and bringing excitement to your kitchen.

Within these pages, you will find a wide array of tantalizing recipes, each designed to make the most of your Ninja Dual Zone Air Fryer. From crispy appetizers to succulent main courses and delectable desserts, there is something to please every palate and occasion. Whether you are a seasoned chef or a cooking enthusiast, we believe you will find inspiration and delight in these recipes.

Our goal is to inspire you to embrace the versatility of your Ninja Dual Zone Air Fryer and embark on countless culinary adventures.
So, grab your apron, preheat your air fryer, and let the magic unfold!
Happy cooking!

Author

After extensive research into our users' cooking habits, we have noticed that this type of book tends to become soiled and repurchased frequently. Therefore, we made a conscious decision to protect the environment and offer our customers an affordable selling price. We understand the significance of reducing environmental pollution, so we have provided the option to print in black and white at a reasonable cost.

Customer satisfaction is our top priority, and we sincerely appreciate your choice to purchase our book. We have meticulously tested and compiled these recipes; however, we acknowledge that a small percentage of customers may not be entirely satisfied. In such instances, we kindly request your understanding and continued support in the future.

Table of Content

Chapter 1: All About Ninja Dual Zone Air Fryer

Chapter 2: Breakfasts

Chapter 3: Family Favorites

Chapter 4: Fast and Easy Everyday Favourites

Chapter 5: Poultry

Chapter 6: Beef, Pork, and Lamb

Chapter 7: Fish and Seafood

Chapter 8: Snacks and Appetizers

Chapter 9: Vegetables and Sides

Chapter 10: Vegetarian Mains

Chapter 11: Desserts

Chapter 1: All About Ninja Dual Zone Air Fryer

Before into the recipes, let's get to know the Ninja Dual Zone Air Fryer. This cookbook provides essential informa- tion about air frying, including its benefits and how to use effectively. Get ready to discover new, healthier, and more convenient of cooking in Ninja Dual Zone Air Fryer.

What is Ninja Dual Zone Air Fryer?

- Air fryers were introduced in the early 2000s as a healthier alternative to deep frying, using hot air to cook food. They have become popular and now come in many brands and styles, used for a variety of foods from appetizers to desserts.

- The Ninja Dual Zone Air Fryer is a new model of air fryer produced by SharkNinja Operating LLC, a manufacturer of household appliances, first introduced in 2020. Although air fryers have been around for over a decade, the Ninja Dual Zone Air Fryer stands out with its dual-zone cooking technology, allowing users to cook two separate dishes at different temperatures and times. This feature makes it a versatile appliance for cooking meals for families or busy individuals. The Ninja Dual Zone Air Fryer has a range of cooking functions, including air frying, roast, reheat, dehydrating, and bake - a versatile and multifunctional device.

- Since its release, the Ninja Dual Zone Air Fryer has received positive reviews for its performance and ease of use, becoming a popular choice for consumers looking for a high-quality air fryer with advanced features. As air frying continues to become more popular as a healthier, the Ninja Dual Zone Air Fryer has the potential to spark a new trend in convenient cooking for UK family.

What Makes the Ninja Dual Zone Air Fryer Stand Out ?

- Dual Zone Cooking: As the name suggests, this air fryer has two cooking zones that allow you to cook two different dishes simultaneously at different temperatures and for different duration in each zone.

- Large Capacity: With a from 6.5-quart capacity, the Ninja Dual Zone Air Fryer can hold more food than many other air fryers on the market, making it great for families or entertaining.

- Precision Cooking: The air fryer comes with custom temperature control, giving you the ability to select temperatures in 5°C increments from 105°C to 230°C, ensuring precision cooking for a variety of meals and snacks.

- Multiple Cooking Functions : The Ninja Dual Zone Air Fryer can do more than just air fry - it can also roast, broil, reheat, and dehydrate. The Ninja Dual Zone Air Fryer also comes with multiple pre-programmed cooking settings for different foods like fries, chicken, vegetables, and more, making it easy for you to cook a variety of dishes with just a touch of a button.

- Easy to Clean: The cooking basket and crisper plate are both non-stick and dishwasher safe, making cleanup quick and effortless.

- Smart Finish Feature: This feature ensures that both zones finish cooking at the same time, making meal planning and prep much easier.

- Healthier Cooking: The air fryer uses up to 75% less fat than traditional frying methods, making it a healthier alternative for those who still crave the taste and texture of fried foods.

- Sleek Design: The Ninja Dual Zone Air Fryer has a modern, sleek design that will complement any kitchen décor.

Air Fryer FAQs and Tricks for the Ninja Dual Zone Air Fryer

Can I adjust the cook time and/or temperature once the unit is running?	Yes. you can adjust the cook time or temperature at any point throughout the cooking process by using the up and down TIME and/or TEMP arrows.
How much can I fill the drawers?	There is no fill line. Make sure that the drawer can close properly in the unit.
Do I need to defrost frozen foods before air frying them?	It depends on the food. Follow package instructions.
Will the outside of the unit get hot?	Although the outside of the unit will heat up during the cooking process, the control panel and air fry drawer handle will remain safe to touch.
Can I air fry wet, battered ingredients?	Yes, but use the proper breading technique. It is important to coat foods first with flour, then with egg, and then with bread crumbs. Press breading firmly onto the battered ingredients, so crumbs won't be blown off by the fan.
Can I pull out the drawers to check on food during cooking?	Yes. We recommend checking on your food regularly throughout the cooking process. Simply pull out the drawer and shake or rotate the food. The timer will pause automatically and the heater and fan will shut off when the drawer is removed. When you are done, slide the drawer back into place. The timer will start and the unit will automatically resume cooking.
Can I cook different foods in each zone and not worry about cross contamination?	Yes, both zones are self-contained with separate heating elements and fans.
Does the unit need to preheat?	The unit does not need to be preheated.
Do I need to use oil when air frying?	Although oil is not required, we recommend starting with one tablespoon and adjusting for personal preference, or referencing the recipe for recommended oil amounts.
Can I use parchment paper or aluminum foil in the air fry drawer?	Yes. It is safe to use parchment paper and aluminum foil in the drawer. The use of aluminum foil is suggested in some recipes.
Is the air fry drawer non-stick?	Yes. The drawers have a PTFE coating.
What materials are the drawers, crisper plate, and unit's exterior made of?	The drawer and crisper plate are made of aluminum with a PTFE coating. The unit's exterior uses FDA-approved food-safe plastic.
What are the timer increments?	The timer increments vary depending on the function: • Air Fry: 1-minute increments up to 1 hour • Roast: 1-minute increments for the first hour, followed by 5-minute increments for the next 3 hours • Dehydrate: 15-minute increments up to 12 hours • Reheat: 1-minute increments up to 1 hour • Bake: 1-minute increments for the first 30 minutes, followed by 5-minute increments for the next 3 1/2 hours • Max Crisp (not included on all models): 1-minute increments up to 30 minutes
What is the temperature range of the unit?	The temperature ranges from 40°C (for Dehydrate) to 240°C (for Max Crisp). Roast, Air Fry, Reheat,and Bake only goes up to 210°C.
What is Max Crisp?	Max Crisp Technology provides hotter, faster, and crispier results for all your favorite prepackaged frozen foods. Max Crisp cooks at 240°C. For best results, reduce cook times and shake food often.
How many cooking functions are included with the unit?	The unit has 6 different cooking functions: Max Crisp, Air Fry, Dehydrate, Roast, Bake, and Reheat
How much food can I cook in each drawer?	Each 3.8L cooking drawer fits up to 1kg of fries or a whole 1.6kg chicken.

FUNCTION BUTTONS

MAX CRISP: Best for frozen foods such as French fries and chicken nuggets.

AIR FRY: Use this function to give your food crispiness and crunch with little to no oil.

ROAST: Use the unit as an oven for tender meats and more.

REHEAT: Revive leftovers by gently warming them, leaving you with crispy results.

DEHYDRATE: Dehydrate meats, fruits and vegetables for healthy snacks.

BAKE: Create decadent baked treats and desserts.

TEMP arrows: Use the up and down arrows to adjust the cook temperature before or during cooking.

TIME arrows: Use the up and down arrows to adjust the cook time in any function before or during the cook cycle.

SYNC button: Automatically syncs the cook times to ensure both zones finish at the same time, even if if they have different cook times.

MATCH button: Automatically matches zone 2 settings to those of zone 1 to cook a larger amount of the same food, or cook different foods using the same function, temperature, and time.

START/STOP button: After selecting temperature and time, start cooking by pressing the START/STOP button.

Power button: The button turns the unit on, and also shuts it off and stops all cooking functions.

STANDBY MODE: After 10 minutes with no interaction with the control panel, the unit will enter standby mode.

HOLD MODE: Hold will appear on the unit while in SYNC mode. One zone will be cooking, while the other zone will be holding until the times sync together.

HELPFUL TIPS

1. For consistent browning, make sure ingredients are arranged in an even layer on the bottom of the drawer with no overlapping. If ingredients are overlapping, make sure to shake them halfway through the set cook time.

2. Cook temperature and time can be adjusted at any time during cooking. Simply select the zone you want to adjust, then press the TEMP arrows to adjust the temperature or the TIME arrows to adjust the time.

3. To convert recipes from your conventional oven, reduce the temperature by 10°C. Check food frequently to avoid overcooking.

4. Occasionally, the fan from the air fryer will blow lightweight foods around. To alleviate this, secure foods (like the top slice of bread on a sandwich) with cocktail sticks.

5. The crisper plates elevate ingredients in the drawers so air can circulate under and around ingredients for even, crisp results.

6. After selecting a cooking function, you can press the START/STOP button to begin cooking immediately. The unit will run at the default temperature and time.

7. For best results with fresh vegetables and potatoes, use at least 1 tablespoon of oil. Add more oil as desired to achieve the preferred level of crispiness.

8. For best results, check progress throughout cooking and remove food when desired level of brownness has been achieved. We recommend using an instant-read thermometer to monitor the internal temperature of meat & fish. After the cook time is complete, remove food immediately to avoid overcooking.

9. For best results, remove food immediately after the cook time is complete to avoid overcooking.

Cooking Measurement Equivalents

Measurement	Abbreviation	Equivalent
Teaspoon	tsp	5 ml
Dessertspoon	dsp	10 ml
Tablespoon	tbsp	15 ml
Fluid ounce	fl oz	28.4 ml
Cup	-	240 ml
Pint	pt	568 ml
Quart	qt	1.14 L
Gallon	gal	4.55 L
Ounce	oz	28 g
Pound	lb	454 g
Milliliter	ml	1/1000 L
Gram	g	1/1000 kg
Inch	in	2.54 cm

Temperature Conversion

Celsius	Fahrenheit
100°C	212°F
110°C	230°F
120°C	250°F
140°C	284°F
150°C	300°F
160°C	320°F
175°C	350°F
180°C	356°F
200°C	392°F
220°C	428°F
240°C	464°F

Key points to effectively use this cookbook:

1. We use the average capacity of Ninja Dual Zone Air Fryer models to write our recipes.Therefore, if one of the cooking instructions is for one zone but it doesn't fit in a single zone of your air fryer, divide it and cook it on two zones, and vice versa. The temperature and time still follow our provided formulas.

2. The MATCH button is frequently used to duplicate settings across both zones. However, don't forget about the SYNC button when you want to cook two separate dishes and serve them simultaneously.

Chapter 2: Breakfasts

EGG IN A HOLE | SERVES 1

Prep time: 5 min | Cook time: 8 min

- 1 slice of bread (white or wholemeal)
- 1 medium egg
- Butter or cooking spray
- Salt and pepper to taste
- Optional toppings: grated cheese, chopped herbs (such as chives or parsley)

DIRECTIONS:

1. Use a round cookie cutter or a glass to cut a hole in the center of the bread slice.
2. Lightly butter or spray both sides of the bread slice with cooking spray.
3. Place the bread slice in Zone 1 of the Air Fryer.
4. Crack the egg into a small bowl, being careful to keep the yolk intact.
5. Gently pour the egg into the hole in the bread slice.
6. Season the egg with salt and pepper to taste.
7. Optionally, sprinkle grated cheese or chopped herbs on top of the bread and egg.
8. Insert the drawer into Zone 1 of the Air Fryer.
9. Select the AIR FRY program, set the temperature to 180°C, and set the time to 8 minutes.
10. Press START/STOP to begin cooking.
11. After 4 minutes, carefully remove the drawer from Zone 1.
12. Check the doneness of the egg. For a runny yolk, cook for less time; for a fully cooked yolk, cook for a longer time.
13. If necessary, return the drawer to Zone 1 and continue cooking until the desired level of doneness is reached.
14. Once cooked to your liking, carefully remove the drawer from the Air Fryer.
15. Serve the **Egg in a Hole** immediately with a side of crispy toast or other preferred accompaniments.

NUTTY GRANOLA | SERVES 4

Prep time: 10 min | Cook time: 15 min

- 200g rolled oats
- 75g mixed nuts (such as almonds, walnuts, and cashews), roughly chopped
- 50g sunflower seeds
- 50g pumpkin seeds
- 2 tablespoons honey or maple syrup
- 2 tablespoons coconut oil, melted
- 1 teaspoon vanilla extract
- 1/2 teaspoon ground cinnamon
- Pinch of salt
- 75g dried fruits (such as raisins, cranberries, or chopped apricots)

DIRECTIONS:

1. In a large bowl, combine the rolled oats, mixed nuts, sunflower seeds, and pumpkin seeds.
2. In a separate small bowl, whisk together the honey or maple syrup, melted coconut oil, vanilla extract, ground cinnamon, and salt.
3. Pour the wet mixture over the dry ingredients in the large bowl. Stir until all the dry ingredients are coated with the wet mixture.
4. Divide the granola mixture evenly between the two zones in the Air Fryer.
5. Select Zone 1, choose the AIR FRY program, and set the temperature to 160°C. Set the time to 15 minutes.
6. Select MATCH to duplicate settings across both zones. Press START/STOP to begin cooking.
7. After 7-8 minutes of cooking time, carefully remove both drawers from the Air Fryer.
8. Shake the drawers to ensure even cooking and prevent any sticking.
9. Return the drawers to the Air Fryer and continue cooking for the remaining time.
10. Once the cooking time is complete, remove both drawers from the Air Fryer and allow the granola to cool completely.
11. Transfer the **Nutty Granola** to an airtight container for storage.

BREAKFAST COBBLER | SERVES 4

Prep time: 15 min | Cook time: 25 min

- 500g mixed berries (such as strawberries, blueberries, and raspberries)
- 2 tablespoons granulated sugar
- 1 tablespoon lemon juice
- 150g self-raising flour
- 50g granulated sugar
- 75g unsalted butter, cold and cubed
- 75ml milk
- 1 teaspoon vanilla extract
- 1 large egg
- Clotted cream or whipped cream, for serving (optional)

DIRECTIONS

1. In a bowl, combine the mixed berries, 2 tablespoons of sugar, and lemon juice. Toss gently to coat the berries in the sugar and lemon juice mixture.
2. In a separate bowl, mix the self-raising flour and 50g of sugar together.
3. Add the cold, cubed butter to the flour mixture. Use your fingers to rub the butter into the flour until the mixture resembles coarse breadcrumbs.
4. In a small jug, whisk together the milk, vanilla extract, and egg.
5. Pour the milk mixture into the flour mixture. Stir until just combined. Be careful not to overmix.
6. Divide the mixed berries evenly among four individual ramekins or oven-safe dishes.
7. Spoon the cobbler batter over the berries, dividing it equally among the ramekins.
8. Insert the ramekins into Zone 1 of the Air Fryer.
9. Select Zone 1, choose the BAKE program, and set the temperature to 180°C. Set the time to 25 minutes.
10. Press START/STOP to begin cooking.
11. After 20 minutes of cooking time, check the cobbler for doneness. The top should be golden brown, and the berries should be bubbling.
12. If needed, continue cooking for an additional 5 minutes or until the cobbler is cooked to your desired level.
13. Carefully remove the ramekins from the Air Fryer using oven mitts or tongs.
14. Allow the cobbler to cool for a few minutes before serving.
15. Serve the **Breakfast Cobbler** warm with a dollop of clotted cream or whipped cream, if desired.

SAVORY SWEET POTATO HASH | SERVES 6

Prep time: 15 min | Cook time: 20 min

- 2 large sweet potatoes, peeled and diced
- 1 red bell pepper, diced
- 1 green bell pepper, diced
- 1 red onion, diced
- 2 cloves of garlic, minced
- 2 tablespoons olive oil
- 1 teaspoon smoked paprika
- 1/2 teaspoon dried thyme
- 1/2 teaspoon dried rosemary
- Salt and pepper to taste
- Fresh parsley or chives, chopped (for garnish)

DIRECTIONS:

1. In a large bowl, combine the diced sweet potatoes, red bell pepper, green bell pepper, red onion, minced garlic, olive oil, smoked paprika, dried thyme, dried rosemary, salt, and pepper. Toss until all the ingredients are well coated.
2. Divide the sweet potato mixture between the two zones in the Air Fryer. Insert both drawers into the unit.
3. Select Zone 1, choose the AIR FRY program, and set the temperature to 200°C. Set the time to 20 minutes. Select MATCH. Press START/STOP to begin cooking.
4. After 10 minutes of cooking time, carefully remove both drawers from the Air Fryer.
5. Shake the drawers to ensure even cooking and prevent any sticking.
6. Return the drawers to the Air Fryer and continue cooking for the remaining time.
7. Once the cooking time is complete, remove both drawers from the Air Fryer.
8. Transfer the **Savory Sweet Potato Hash** to a serving dish and garnish with fresh parsley or chives.
9. Serve the hash as a delicious side dish for breakfast, brunch, or alongside your favorite main course.

CHEESY SCRAMBLED EGGS | SERVES 2

Prep time: 5 min | Cook time: 5 min

- 4 large eggs
- 50ml milk
- 50g grated cheddar cheese
- 1 tablespoon unsalted butter
- Salt and pepper to taste
- Fresh chives or parsley, chopped (for garnish)

DIRECTIONS:

1. Preheat the Ninja Dual Zone Air Fryer in Zone 1 to 180°C.
2. In a bowl, crack the eggs and whisk them together with the milk until well combined.
3. Stir in the grated cheddar cheese and season with salt and pepper.
4. In Zone 1 of the Air Fryer, melt the butter.
5. Once the butter is melted, pour in the egg mixture.
6. Select Zone 1, choose the AIR FRY program, and set the temperature to 180°C. Set the time to 5 minutes.
7. Press START/STOP to begin cooking.
8. After 2 minutes of cooking time, open the drawer and gently stir the eggs with a silicone spatula to scramble them.
9. Close the drawer and continue cooking for the remaining time.
10. When the cooking time is complete, remove the drawer from the Air Fryer.
11. Let the eggs rest for a minute before serving.
12. Sprinkle with fresh chives or parsley for garnish.
13. Serve the **Cheesy Scrambled Eggs** hot with toast, fried mushrooms, or grilled tomatoes for a complete breakfast.

BLUEBERRY COBBLER & BREAKFAST CALZONE | SERVES 4

Prep time: 30 min | Cook time: 25 min

BLUEBERRY COBBLER:

- 500g blueberries
- 2 tablespoons granulated sugar
- 1 tablespoon lemon juice
- 150g self-raising flour
- 50g granulated sugar
- 75g unsalted butter, cold and cubed
- 75ml milk
- 1 teaspoon vanilla extract
- Clotted cream or whipped cream, for serving (optional)

DIRECTIONS:

1. In a bowl, combine the blueberries, 2 tablespoons of sugar, and lemon juice. Toss gently to coat the blueberries in the sugar and lemon juice mixture.
2. In a separate bowl, mix the self-raising flour and 50g of sugar together.
3. Add the cold, cubed butter to the flour mixture. Use your fingers to rub the butter into the flour until the mixture resembles coarse breadcrumbs.
4. In a small jug, whisk together the milk and vanilla extract.
5. Pour the milk mixture into the flour mixture. Stir until just combined. Be careful not to overmix.
6. Divide the blueberries evenly among four individual ramekins or oven-safe dishes.
7. Spoon the cobbler batter over the blueberries, dividing it equally among the ramekins.
8. Insert the ramekins into Zone 1 of the Air Fryer.
9. Select Zone 1, choose the BAKE program, and set the temperature to 180°C. Set the time to 25 minutes.
10. Press START/STOP to begin cooking.
11. After 20 minutes of cooking time, check the cobbler for doneness. The top should be golden brown, and the blueberries should be bubbling.
12. If needed, continue cooking for an additional 5 minutes or until the cobbler is cooked to your desired level.
13. Allow the **cobbler** to cool for a few minutes before serving.

BREAKFAST CALZONE:

- 1 sheet ready-made puff pastry, thawed
- 4 large eggs
- 100g cooked bacon, chopped
- 100g grated cheddar cheese
- Salt and pepper to taste
- Fresh parsley or chives, chopped (for garnish)

DIRECTIONS:

1. Roll out the puff pastry sheet and cut it into 4 equal squares.
2. Place each square of puff pastry on a separate piece of parchment paper.
3. In the center of each puff pastry square, crack an egg.
4. Sprinkle the cooked bacon and grated cheddar cheese over the eggs.
5. Season with salt and pepper to taste.
6. Fold the corners of the puff pastry square over the filling, forming a sealed calzone shape. Place the calzones with the parchment paper in Zone 2 of the Air Fryer.
7. Select Zone 2, choose the AIR FRY program, and set the temperature to 200°C. Set the time to 15 minutes.
8. Press START/STOP to begin cooking.
9. After 15 minutes of cooking time, check the **Calzone**. If needed, continue cooking for an additional 5 minutes or until the Calzone is cooked to your desired level.
10. Let cool for a few minutes before serving.

> If you would like to serve both Cobbler and Calzone simultaneously: Prepare the ingredients for both dishes and place them in their respective zones, choose the cooking program and time for each zone, and then select **SYNC**

HEARTY CHEDDAR BISCUITS | MAKES 8 BISCUITS

Prep time: 15 min | Cook time: 10 min

- 225g self-raising flour
- 1 teaspoon baking powder
- 1/2 teaspoon salt
- 50g unsalted butter, cold and cubed
- 100g grated cheddar cheese
- 150ml milk
- 1 tablespoon chopped fresh chives or spring onions (optional)
- 1 tablespoon melted butter, for brushing (optional)

DIRECTIONS:

1. In a large bowl, mix together the self-raising flour, baking powder, and salt.
2. Add the cold, cubed butter to the flour mixture. Use your fingers to rub the butter into the flour until the mixture resembles coarse breadcrumbs.
3. Stir in the grated cheddar cheese and chopped fresh chives or spring onions, if using.
4. Gradually pour in the milk while stirring the mixture. Mix until the dough comes together. Be careful not to overmix.
5. Turn the dough out onto a floured surface and gently knead it a few times until it becomes smooth.
6. Roll out the dough to a thickness of about 2cm.
7. Use a round biscuit cutter to cut out 8 biscuits from the dough.
8. Place the biscuits in Zone 1 of the Air Fryer.
9. Select Zone 1, choose the BAKE program, and set the temperature to 180°C. Set the time to 10 minutes.
10. Press START/STOP to begin cooking.
11. After 8 minutes of cooking time, open the drawer and brush the tops of the biscuits with melted butter, if desired. This step will give them a golden, glossy finish.
12. Close the drawer and continue cooking for the remaining time.
13. When the cooking time is complete, remove the drawer from the Air Fryer.
14. Allow the biscuits to cool slightly before serving.
15. Serve the **Hearty Cheddar Biscuits** warm as a delightful accompaniment to soups, stews, or enjoyed on their own as a tasty snack.

CHEDDAR EGGS | SERVES 2

Prep time: 5 min | Cook time: 10 min

- 4 large eggs
- 50g cheddar cheese, grated
- 2 tablespoons milk
- Salt and pepper to taste
- Fresh chives or parsley, chopped (for garnish)

DIRECTIONS:

1. In a bowl, whisk together the eggs, grated cheddar cheese, milk, salt, and pepper until well combined.
2. Pour the egg mixture into a greased or lined baking dish that fits in Zone 1 of the Air Fryer.
3. Place the baking dish in Zone 1 of the Air Fryer.
4. Select Zone 1, choose the BAKE program, and set the temperature to 180°C. Set the time to 10 minutes.
5. Press START/STOP to begin cooking.
6. When the cooking time is complete, remove the baking dish from the Air Fryer using oven mitts or tongs, as it will be hot.
7. Let the **Cheddar Eggs** cool for a minute or two, then sprinkle with chopped fresh chives or parsley for garnish.
8. Serve the Cheddar Eggs hot with toast or crusty bread.

CINNAMON ROLLS | MAKES 12 ROLLS

Prep time: 30 min | Cook time: 12 min

For the dough:
- 500g strong white bread flour
- 7g instant yeast
- 50g granulated sugar
- 1 teaspoon salt
- 250ml warm milk
- 50g unsalted butter, melted
- 1 large egg

For the filling:
- 75g unsalted butter, softened
- 150g light brown sugar
- 2 tablespoons ground cinnamon

For the glaze:
- 200g icing sugar
- 2-3 tablespoons milk
- 1 teaspoon vanilla extract

DIRECTIONS

1. In a large mixing bowl, combine the bread flour, instant yeast, granulated sugar, and salt.
2. Make a well in the center of the dry ingredients and pour in the warm milk, melted butter, and egg.
3. Mix the ingredients together until a dough forms.
4. Turn the dough out onto a floured surface and knead for about 5 minutes until smooth and elastic.
5. Place the dough back in the bowl, cover with a clean kitchen towel, and let it rest for 10 minutes.
6. Roll out the dough into a rectangle approximately 30cm x 40cm in size.
7. Spread the softened butter evenly over the dough.
8. In a small bowl, mix together the light brown sugar and ground cinnamon. Sprinkle this mixture over the buttered dough, covering it completely.
9. Starting from one long side, tightly roll the dough into a log shape.
10. Cut the log into 12 equal-sized rolls. Place 6 rolls in each zone of the air fryer.
11. Select Zone 1, choose the BAKE program, and set the temperature to 180°C. Set the time to 12 minutes. Select MATCH. Press START/STOP to begin cooking.
12. While the rolls are cooking, prepare the glaze by whisking together the icing sugar, milk, and vanilla extract until smooth.
13. After the cooking time is complete, remove drawers from the Air Fryer and let the rolls cool for a few minutes.
14. Drizzle the glaze over the warm cinnamon rolls.
15. Serve the **Cinnamon Rolls** while still warm and enjoy their sweet, spiced goodness.

APPLE ROLLS | MAKES 12 ROLLS

Prep time: 30 min | Cook time: 12 min

For the dough:
- 500g strong white bread flour
- 7g instant yeast
- 50g granulated sugar
- 1 teaspoon salt
- 250ml warm milk
- 50g unsalted butter, melted
- 1 large egg

For the filling:
- 4 apples, peeled, cored, and diced
- 50g unsalted butter
- 75g light brown sugar
- 1 teaspoon ground cinnamon

For the glaze:
- 200g icing sugar
- 2-3 tablespoons milk
- 1 teaspoon vanilla extract

DIRECTIONS

1. In a large mixing bowl, combine the bread flour, instant yeast, granulated sugar, and salt.
2. Make a well in the center of the dry ingredients and pour in the warm milk, melted butter, and egg.
3. Mix the ingredients together until a dough forms.
4. Turn the dough out onto a floured surface and knead for about 5 minutes until smooth and elastic.
5. Place the dough back in the bowl, cover with a clean kitchen towel, and let it rest for 10 minutes.
6. In a saucepan, melt the butter over medium heat. Add the diced apples, light brown sugar, and ground cinnamon. Cook until the apples are softened and caramelized, about 5-7 minutes. Remove from heat and let it cool.
7. Roll out the dough into a rectangle approximately 30cm x 40cm in size.
8. Spread the caramelized apple mixture evenly over the dough.
9. Starting from one long side, tightly roll the dough into a log shape.
10. Cut the log into 12 equal-sized rolls. Place 6 rolls in each zone of the air fryer.
11. Select Zone 1, choose the BAKE program, and set the temperature to 180°C. Set the time to 12 minutes. Select MATCH. Press START/STOP to begin cooking.
12. While the rolls are cooking, prepare the glaze by whisking together the icing sugar, milk, and vanilla extract until smooth.
13. After the cooking time is complete, remove drawers from the Air Fryer and let the rolls cool for a few minutes.
14. Drizzle the glaze over the warm apple rolls.
15. Serve the **Apple Rolls** while still warm and enjoy the delicious combination of soft, sweet dough and caramelized apple filling.

FRIED CHICKEN WINGS WITH WAFFLES | SERVES 4

Prep time: 15 min | Cook time: 25 min

For the Chicken Wings:
- 800g chicken wings
- 150g all-purpose flour
- 1 teaspoon paprika
- 1 teaspoon garlic powder
- 1 teaspoon onion powder
- 1/2 teaspoon salt
- 1/4 teaspoon black pepper
- Vegetable oil, for spraying

For the Waffles:
- 200g plain flour
- 2 tablespoons granulated sugar
- 1 tablespoon baking powder
- 1/2 teaspoon salt
- 300ml milk
- 2 large eggs
- 60g unsalted butter, melted
- Vegetable oil, for spraying

For Serving:
- Maple syrup
- Butter

DIRECTIONS

1. In a mixing bowl, combine the flour, paprika, garlic powder, onion powder, salt, and black pepper for the chicken wings coating.
2. Dip each chicken wing into the flour mixture, coating it evenly. Shake off any excess flour.
3. Place the coated chicken wings in Zone 1 of the Air Fryer.
4. Select Zone 1, choose the AIR FRY program, and set the temperature to 200°C. Set the time to 25 minutes.
5. Press START/STOP to begin cooking.
6. While the chicken wings are cooking, prepare the waffle batter. In a separate bowl, whisk together the flour, sugar, baking powder, and salt for the waffles.
7. In another bowl, whisk together the milk, eggs, and melted butter. Pour the wet ingredients into the dry ingredients and mix until just combined.
8. Lightly grease the waffle plates in Zone 2 of the Air Fryer with cooking spray or melted butter.
9. Pour the waffle batter onto the greased plates, spreading it out evenly.
10. Close the Air Fryer and select the BAKE program for Zone 2. Set the temperature to 180°C and the cooking time to 10-12 minutes.
11. Cook until the waffles are golden brown and cooked through.
12. Remove the cooked chicken wings and waffles from the Air Fryer.
13. Serve the crispy fried chicken wings with the freshly made waffles.
14. Top with a pat of butter and drizzle with maple syrup.
15. Enjoy the delicious combination of **crispy chicken wings and fluffy waffles**!

SAUSAGE EGG CUP | SERVES 6

Prep time: 10 min | Cook time: 15 min

- 6 large eggs
- 6 sausage links (pork or chicken)
- 1/2 red bell pepper, diced
- 1/2 green bell pepper, diced
- 1/2 onion, diced
- 100g cheddar cheese, grated
- Salt and pepper to taste
- Fresh parsley, chopped (for garnish)

DIRECTIONS:

1. In a skillet, cook the sausage links over medium heat until browned and fully cooked. Remove from the skillet and let them cool slightly.
2. Cut the cooked sausages into small pieces.
3. In a bowl, whisk the eggs until well beaten. Season with salt and pepper.
4. Grease or line six individual ramekins or silicone cupcake liners.
5. Divide the diced bell peppers, onion, cooked sausage pieces, and grated cheddar cheese among the ramekins.
6. Pour the beaten eggs evenly into each ramekin, covering the ingredients.
7. Place 3 ramekins in each zone of the air fryer.
8. Select Zone 1, choose the BAKE program, and set the temperature to 180°C. Set the time to 15 minutes. Select MATCH. Press START/STOP to begin cooking.
9. When the cooking time is complete, remove the ramekins from the Air Fryer using oven mitts or tongs, as they will be hot.
10. Let the Sausage Egg Cups cool for a minute or two, then sprinkle with fresh parsley for garnish.
11. Serve the **Sausage Egg Cups** hot as a delicious breakfast or brunch option.

BUNLESS BREAKFAST TURKEY BURGERS | SERVES 4

Prep time: 15 min | Cook time: 20 min

- 500g ground turkey
- 1/2 onion, finely chopped
- 1/2 red bell pepper, finely chopped
- 2 cloves garlic, minced
- 1 teaspoon dried thyme
- 1 teaspoon dried sage
- 1/2 teaspoon paprika
- Salt and pepper to taste
- 4 large eggs
- 4 slices cheddar cheese
- Fresh lettuce leaves
- Sliced tomatoes
- Sliced avocado
- Ketchup or your preferred sauce (optional)
- Olive oil, for spraying

DIRECTIONS:

1. In a mixing bowl, combine the ground turkey, chopped onion, chopped red bell pepper, minced garlic, dried thyme, dried sage, paprika, salt, and pepper. Mix until well combined.
2. Divide the turkey mixture into four equal portions and shape them into patties.
3. Spray the patties with olive oil to help them brown and prevent sticking.
4. Place the turkey patties in Zone 1 of the Air Fryer.
5. Select Zone 1, choose the AIR FRY program, and set the temperature to 200°C. Set the time to 20 minutes. Press START/STOP to begin cooking.
6. While the turkey burgers are cooking, prepare the eggs. In Zone 2 of the Air Fryer, crack the eggs and season with salt and pepper.
7. Select Zone 2, choose the AIR FRY program, and set the temperature to 180°C. Set the time to 5 minutes. Press START/STOP to begin cooking the eggs.
8. When the cooking time for the turkey burgers is almost finished, place a slice of cheddar cheese on each patty and let it melt slightly.
9. Remove the turkey burgers and eggs from the Air Fryer.
10. Assemble the bunless turkey burgers by placing each patty on a lettuce leaf.
11. Top with a fried egg, sliced tomatoes, sliced avocado, and any other desired toppings.
12. Serve the **bunless breakfast turkey burgers** with ketchup or your preferred sauce, if desired.

CINNAMON-RAISIN BAGELS | MAKES 4 BAGELS

Prep time: 20 min | Cook time: 15 min

- 300g bread flour
- 1 1/2 teaspoons instant yeast
- 1 tablespoon granulated sugar
- 1/2 teaspoon salt
- 1/2 teaspoon ground cinnamon
- 100g raisins
- 180ml warm water
- 1 tablespoon honey
- 1 tablespoon boiling water
- 1 egg, beaten (for egg wash)

DIRECTIONS:

1. In a large mixing bowl, combine the bread flour, instant yeast, granulated sugar, salt, ground cinnamon, and raisins.
2. Make a well in the center and pour in the warm water. Mix with a wooden spoon or your hands until a dough forms.
3. Transfer the dough to a lightly floured surface and knead for about 5-7 minutes until smooth and elastic.
4. Divide the dough into 4 equal portions and shape each portion into a ball. Flatten the balls slightly to form bagel shapes with a hole in the center.
5. In a small bowl, dissolve the honey in boiling water. Brush the bagels with the honey-water mixture using a pastry brush.
6. Preheat the Ninja Dual Zone Air Fryer in Zone 1 to 200°C.
7. Place the bagels on a parchment-lined tray and transfer them to Zone 1 of the Air Fryer.
8. Select Zone 1, choose the BAKE program, and set the temperature to 200°C. Set the time to 15 minutes.
9. Press START/STOP to begin cooking.
10. After 8 minutes of cooking, remove the tray from the Air Fryer and brush the bagels with beaten egg wash.
11. Return the tray to the Air Fryer and continue cooking for the remaining 7 minutes.
12. When the cooking time is complete, remove the bagels from the Air Fryer and let them cool on a wire rack.
13. Serve the **cinnamon-raisin bagels** and enjoy them plain or with your favorite spreads.

CAJUN BREAKFAST SAUSAGE | SERVES 8

Prep time: 10 min | Cook time: 15 min

- 500g ground pork
- 1 tablespoon Cajun seasoning
- 1/2 teaspoon garlic powder
- 1/2 teaspoon onion powder
- 1/2 teaspoon dried thyme
- 1/2 teaspoon dried oregano
- 1/2 teaspoon paprika
- 1/4 teaspoon cayenne pepper (adjust to taste)
- Salt and pepper to taste
- Olive oil, for spraying

DIRECTIONS:

1. In a mixing bowl, combine the ground pork, Cajun seasoning, garlic powder, onion powder, dried thyme, dried oregano, paprika, cayenne pepper, salt, and pepper. Mix well to ensure the seasonings are evenly distributed.
2. Divide the mixture into 8 equal portions and shape each portion into a sausage patty.
3. Evenly dividing them between the two zone. Select Zone 1, choose the AIR FRY program, and set the temperature to 200°C. Set the time to 15 minutes.
4. Select MATCH to duplicate settings across both zones. Press START/STOP to begin cooking.
5. After 7 minutes of cooking, flip the sausage patties using tongs to ensure even browning.
6. Spray the patties with a little olive oil to help them crisp up.
7. Return the trays to the Air Fryer and continue cooking for the remaining 8 minutes.
8. When the cooking time is complete, remove the sausage patties from the Air Fryer and let them cool for a few minutes.
9. Serve the **Cajun breakfast sausage** patties hot with your preferred breakfast accompaniments.

PIZZA EGGS

Prep time: 10 min | Cook time: 10 min

- 4 large eggs
- 4 tablespoons tomato sauce
- 4 tablespoons grated mozzarella cheese
- 4 tablespoons chopped bell peppers
- 4 tablespoons sliced black olives
- 4 tablespoons sliced mushrooms
- 4 tablespoons sliced pepperoni or cooked bacon
- Salt and pepper, to taste
- Fresh basil leaves, for garnish (optional)

DIRECTIONS:

1. Lightly grease the crisper plate in Zone 1 of the Air Fryer.
2. Crack one egg into each quadrant of the crisper plate, ensuring they are evenly spaced.
3. Spoon 1 tablespoon of tomato sauce over each egg.
4. Sprinkle 1 tablespoon of grated mozzarella cheese over each egg.
5. Top each egg with 1 tablespoon each of chopped bell peppers, sliced black olives, sliced mushrooms, and sliced pepperoni or cooked bacon.
6. Season with salt and pepper to taste.
7. Close the Air Fryer and select the BAKE program for Zone 1. Set the temperature to 180°C and the cooking time to 10 minutes.
8. Cook until the eggs are set and the cheese is melted and bubbly.
9. Carefully remove the crisper plate from the Air Fryer using oven mitts or tongs.
10. Garnish with fresh basil leaves, if desired.
11. Serve the **Pizza Eggs** hot as a delicious and savory breakfast or brunch option.

BACON, BROCCOLI AND CHEESE BREAD PUDDING | SERVES 2 TO 4

Prep time: 10 min | Cook time: 15 min

- 4 slices of bread, preferably stale or day-old
- 4 slices of bacon, cooked and crumbled
- 100g broccoli florets, blanched and chopped
- 100g grated cheddar cheese
- 4 large eggs
- 240ml milk
- 1/2 teaspoon Dijon mustard
- 1/2 teaspoon dried thyme
- Salt and pepper, to taste

DIRECTIONS:

1. Lightly grease a baking dish that fits in Zone 1 of the Air Fryer.
2. Cut the bread slices into cubes and spread them evenly in the greased baking dish.
3. Sprinkle the crumbled bacon, chopped broccoli florets, and grated cheddar cheese over the bread cubes.
4. In a separate bowl, whisk together the eggs, milk, Dijon mustard, dried thyme, salt, and pepper.
5. Pour the egg mixture over the bread mixture in the baking dish, ensuring everything is evenly coated.
6. Place the baking dish in Zone 1 of the Air Fryer.
7. Close the Air Fryer and select the Bake program for Zone 1. Set the temperature to 180°C and the cooking time to 25 minutes.
8. Cook until the bread pudding is golden brown and set in the center.
9. Carefully remove the baking dish from the Air Fryer using oven mitts or tongs.
10. Allow the bread pudding to cool for a few minutes before serving.
11. Serve the **Bacon, Broccoli, and Cheese Bread Pudding** warm as a delicious and satisfying meal.

ASPARAGUS AND BELL PEPPER STRATA | SERVES 4

Prep time: 15 min | Cook time: 25 min

- 6 slices of bread, cubed
- 1 bunch of asparagus, trimmed and cut into bite-sized pieces
- 1 red bell pepper, diced
- 1 yellow bell pepper, diced
- 110g grated cheddar cheese
- 4 large eggs
- 350 ml milk
- 1 teaspoon Dijon mustard
- 1/2 teaspoon dried thyme
- Salt and pepper to taste
- Olive oil, for greasing

DIRECTIONS:

1. Grease the cooking tray in Zone 1 with a little olive oil.
2. In a large bowl, combine the bread cubes, asparagus, bell peppers, and grated cheddar cheese. Mix well.
3. In a separate bowl, whisk together the eggs, milk, Dijon mustard, dried thyme, salt, and pepper.
4. Pour the egg mixture over the bread mixture and stir until all the ingredients are evenly coated.
5. Transfer the mixture to the greased tray in Zone 1 of the Air Fryer.
6. Select Zone 1, choose the BAKE program, and set the temperature to 180°C. Set the time to 25 minutes.
7. Press START/STOP to begin cooking.
8. When the cooking time is complete, carefully remove the tray from the Air Fryer using oven mitts.
9. Allow the strata to cool for a few minutes before serving.
10. Serve the **Asparagus and Bell Pepper Strata** as a delicious and satisfying breakfast or brunch option.

PANCAKE CAKE | SERVES 4

Prep time: 15 min | Cook time: 20 min

- 200g self-raising flour
- 2 tablespoons caster sugar
- 1 teaspoon baking powder
- 1/4 teaspoon salt
- 2 large eggs
- 300ml milk
- 1 teaspoon vanilla extract
- Butter or oil, for greasing
- Desired toppings (e.g., fresh berries, sliced bananas, maple syrup, yogurt)

DIRECTIONS:

1. In a mixing bowl, combine the self-raising flour, caster sugar, baking powder, and salt.
2. In a separate bowl, whisk together the eggs, milk, and vanilla extract until well combined.
3. Gradually pour the wet ingredients into the dry ingredients while whisking continuously, until a smooth batter is formed.
4. Preheat both zones of the Ninja Dual Zone Air Fryer at 180°C.
5. Lightly grease both zones with butter or oil.
6. Divide the pancake batter evenly into 2 halves, pour into 2 zones, spreading it evenly.
7. Close the Air Fryer and select the BAKE program for Zone 1. Set the temperature to 180°C and the cooking time to 10 minutes. Select MATCH. Press START/STOP to begin cooking.
8. While the pancakes are cooking, prepare your desired toppings.
9. Once the pancakes are cooked, carefully remove them from the Air Fryer using a spatula or tongs.
10. Layer the pancakes on a serving plate, adding your desired toppings between each layer.
11. Serve the **Pancake Cake** warm with additional toppings, such as fresh berries, sliced bananas, maple syrup, or yogurt.

PORTOBELLO EGGS BENEDICT | SERVES 2

Prep time: 10 min | Cook time: 15 min

- 2 large Portobello mushrooms
- 2 slices of cooked ham
- 2 large eggs
- 2 English muffins, split and toasted
- Fresh chives or parsley, chopped (for garnish)

Hollandaise sauce:

- 2 large egg yolks
- 1 tablespoon lemon juice
- 100g unsalted butter, melted
- Salt and pepper to taste

Note: If English muffins are not available, we also have a recipe for homemade English muffins on the next page.

DIRECTIONS

1. Remove the stems from the Portobello mushrooms and gently scrape out the gills with a spoon to create a hollow space.
2. Place the mushroom caps in Zone 1 of the Air Fryer and Select AIR FRY. Set the temperature to 180°C and the time to 5 minutes. Press START. The mushrooms will be slightly softened after cooking.
3. While the mushrooms are cooking, prepare the Hollandaise sauce. In a heatproof bowl, whisk together the egg yolks and lemon juice until well combined.
4. Gradually drizzle in the melted butter while whisking constantly until the sauce thickens. Season with salt and pepper to taste.
5. In Zone 2 of the Air Fryer, place the slices of ham and Select AIR FRY. Set the temperature to 180°C and the time to 3 minutes. Press START to warm up the ham slices.
6. Remove the mushroom caps and ham slices from the Air Fryer.
7. To poach the eggs, bring a small saucepan of water to a simmer. Add a splash of vinegar to the water and create a gentle whirlpool with a spoon.
8. Crack each egg into a separate ramekin or small bowl, then carefully slide them into the swirling water. Poach the eggs for about 3-4 minutes until the whites are set but the yolks are still runny.
9. Assemble the Portobello Eggs Benedict by placing a slice of ham on top of each mushroom cap.
10. Place the toasted English muffin halves in Zone 2 of the Air Fryer and Select AIR FRY. Set the temperature to 180°C and the time to 2 minutes. Press START to warm up the English muffins.
11. Remove the English muffins from the Air Fryer and place them on serving plates.
12. Top each English muffin half with a Portobello mushroom cap and ham.
13. Carefully remove the poached eggs from the simmering water with a slotted spoon and place one on top of each mushroom cap.
14. Drizzle Hollandaise sauce generously over the eggs and garnish with chopped chives or parsley.
15. Serve the **Portobello Eggs Benedict.**

ENGLISH MUFFINS | SERVES 4

Prep time: 20 min | Cook time: 15 min

- 450g strong white bread flour
- 1 teaspoon salt
- 2 teaspoons caster sugar
- 2 teaspoons instant yeast
- 225ml warm milk
- 1 tablespoon melted butter
- Semolina or cornmeal, for dusting

DIRECTIONS:

1. In a large mixing bowl, combine the bread flour, salt, caster sugar, and instant yeast.
2. Make a well in the center of the dry ingredients and pour in the warm milk and melted butter.
3. Mix the ingredients together using a wooden spoon until a soft dough forms.
4. Turn the dough out onto a lightly floured surface and knead for about 5 minutes until smooth and elastic.
5. Divide the dough into 4 equal portions and shape each portion into a round ball.
6. Place the dough balls onto a baking tray lined with parchment paper and lightly dusted with semolina or cornmeal.
7. Preheat Zone 1 of the Ninja Dual Zone Air Fryer to Bake at 180°C.
8. Place the baking tray with the dough balls into Zone 1 of the Air Fryer and close the lid.
9. Select Zone 1, choose the BAKE and set the temperature to 180°C. Set the time to 15 minutes.
10. Once they are golden brown and cooked through, remove the English muffins from the Air Fryer and allow them to cool on a wire rack.
11. To serve, split the **English muffins** in half and toast them. They can be enjoyed with butter, jam, or your favorite toppings.

SPINACH OMELET | SERVES 2

Prep time: 10 min | Cook time: 10 min

- 4 large eggs
- 100g fresh spinach leaves
- 50g grated cheddar cheese
- 1 small onion, diced
- 1 tablespoon butter
- Salt and pepper to taste
- Fresh parsley, chopped (for garnish)

DIRECTIONS:

1. In a bowl, beat the eggs and season with salt and pepper.
2. Place the diced onion in Zone 1 of the Air Fryer and select AIR FRY. Set the temperature to 180°C. Cook for about 3-5 minutes until the onion becomes translucent.
3. Add the fresh spinach leaves to Zone 1 of the Air Fryer with the cooked onions. Cook for an additional 2 minutes until the spinach wilts.
4. Transfer the cooked onions and spinach to a separate bowl.
5. In Zone 2 of the Air Fryer, melt the butter using AIR FRY program. Set the temperature to 180°C. Time: 1 minute.
6. Pour the beaten eggs into Zone 2 with the melted butter and cook for 2 minutes, or until the edges start to set.
7. Sprinkle the cooked onions, spinach, and grated cheddar cheese evenly over one half of the omelet in Zone 2.
8. Close the Air Fryer and continue cooking for an additional 3-4 minutes, or until the omelet is cooked through and the cheese has melted.
9. Carefully remove the omelet from the Air Fryer and fold it in half.
10. Garnish with fresh chopped parsley.
11. Serve the **Spinach Omelet** warm as a delicious breakfast or brunch option.

EGG TARTS | MAKES 2 TARTS

Prep time: 15 min | Cook time: 20 min

- 200g ready-made shortcrust pastry
- 2 large eggs
- 100ml double cream
- 30g caster sugar
- 1/2 teaspoon vanilla extract
- Pinch of salt
- Icing sugar (for dusting)

DIRECTIONS:

1. Roll out the shortcrust pastry on a lightly floured surface until it is approximately 3-4mm thick.
2. Cut out two circles of pastry that are slightly larger than your tart molds.
3. Line the tart molds with the pastry circles, gently pressing them into the bottom and sides. Trim any excess pastry.
4. In a mixing bowl, whisk together the eggs, double cream, caster sugar, vanilla extract, and salt until well combined.
5. Pour the egg mixture evenly into the prepared tart molds.
6. Place the filled tart molds in Zone 1 of the Air Fryer and select BAKE. Set the temperature to 180°C
7. Bake for 18-20 minutes, or until the egg tarts are set and the pastry is golden brown.
8. Once cooked, carefully remove the tart molds from the Air Fryer and let them cool for a few minutes.
9. Dust the egg tarts with icing sugar.
10. Serve the **Egg Tarts** warm or chilled as a delightful sweet treat.

RED PEPPER AND FETA FRITTATA | SERVES 4

Prep time: 10 min | Cook time: 18 min

- 6 large eggs
- 100ml milk
- 1 red bell pepper, diced
- 100g feta cheese, crumbled
- 1 small red onion, finely chopped
- Handful of fresh parsley, chopped
- Salt and pepper, to taste
- Olive oil, for greasing

DIRECTIONS:

1. In a large mixing bowl, whisk together the eggs and milk until well combined.
2. Add the diced red bell pepper, crumbled feta cheese, chopped red onion, and fresh parsley to the egg mixture. Season with salt and pepper to taste. Stir until all ingredients are evenly distributed.
3. Lightly grease a baking dish that fits into Zone 1 of the Air Fryer with olive oil.
4. Pour the egg mixture into the greased baking dish, spreading it out evenly.
5. Place the baking dish in Zone 1 of the Air Fryer and select BAKE. Set the temperature to 180°C.
6. Bake for 15-18 minutes, or until the frittata is set and slightly golden on top.
7. Once cooked, carefully remove the baking dish from the Air Fryer and let it cool for a few minutes.
8. Cut the **frittata** into wedges and serve warm as a delicious breakfast or brunch option.

Chapter 3: Family Favorites

CAJUN SHRIMP | SERVES 4

Prep time: 25 min| Cook time: 8 min

- 450g large shrimp, peeled and deveined
- 2 tablespoons olive oil
- 1 tablespoon Cajun seasoning
- 1 teaspoon paprika
- 1 teaspoon garlic powder
- 1/2 teaspoon salt
- 1/4 teaspoon black pepper
- 1/4 teaspoon cayenne pepper (adjust to taste)
- 1 tablespoon fresh lemon juice
- Chopped fresh parsley (for garnish)
- Lemon wedges (for serving)

DIRECTIONS:

1. In a large bowl, combine the olive oil, Cajun seasoning, paprika, garlic powder, salt, black pepper, cayenne pepper, and lemon juice. Mix well to create a marinade.
2. Add the shrimp to the marinade and toss until they are evenly coated. Allow the shrimp to marinate for about 15-20 minutes.
3. Place the marinated shrimp in the cooking basket of one zone.
4. Select the "AIR FRY" program. Set the temperature to 200°C. Set the cooking time to 8 minutes. Press START/STOP to begin cooking. Shake the basket halfway through cooking to ensure even cooking.
5. While the shrimp are cooking, you can prepare a side dish or salad to accompany the meal.
6. Once the shrimp are cooked, remove them from the air fryer and transfer them to a serving dish.
7. Garnish with chopped fresh parsley and serve with lemon wedges on the side for squeezing over the shrimp.
8. Enjoy your delicious **Cajun Shrimp**!

VEGGIE TUNA MELTS | SERVES 4

Prep time: 15 min |Cook time: 10 min

- 2 cans (320g total) tuna, drained
- 100g grated cheddar cheese
- 60g mayonnaise
- 40g finely chopped red onion
- 40g finely chopped celery
- 2 tablespoons chopped fresh parsley
- 1 tablespoon lemon juice
- Salt and pepper to taste
- 4 English muffins, split
- Butter for spreading
- Sliced tomato (optional)
- Sliced cucumber (optional)

DIRECTIONS:

1. In a mixing bowl, combine the drained tuna, grated cheddar cheese, mayonnaise, red onion, celery, parsley, lemon juice, salt, and pepper. Mix well to combine.
2. Spread butter on the cut sides of the English muffins.
3. Place the English muffins in one zone of the air fryer, cut-side up.
4. Select the "AIR FRY" program. Set the temperature to 180°C and set the cooking time to 4 minutes. Press START/STOP to begin cooking.
5. While the English muffins are toasting, spoon the tuna mixture evenly onto the cut sides of the muffins.
6. If desired, add sliced tomato and cucumber on top of the tuna mixture.
7. Once the English muffins are toasted, carefully remove them from the air fryer and place them on a serving plate.
8. Return the loaded English muffins to the air fryer basket, with the tuna side facing up.
9. Select "AIR FRY". Set the cooking time to 4 minutes. Set the temperature to 180°C. Press START/STOP.
10. Cook until the cheese is melted, and the tuna mixture is heated through.
11. Once cooked, remove the Veggie Tuna Melts from the air fryer and serve hot.
12. Enjoy your delicious **Veggie Tuna Melts**!

FISH AND VEGETABLE TACOS | SERVES 4

Prep time: 15 min | Cook time: 15 min

- 4 white fish fillets (such as cod or haddock), about 150g each
- 2 tablespoons olive oil
- 1 tablespoon lime juice
- 1 teaspoon ground cumin
- 1 teaspoon paprika
- 1/2 teaspoon garlic powder
- 1/2 teaspoon chili powder
- Salt and pepper to taste
- 8 small flour tortillas
- 100g shredded lettuce
- 150g sliced bell peppers
- 75g sliced red onion
- Fresh cilantro leaves (for garnish)
- Lime wedges (for serving)

DIRECTIONS:

1. In a bowl, combine the olive oil, lime juice, cumin, paprika, garlic powder, chili powder, salt, and pepper to create a marinade.
2. Place the fish fillets in the marinade and ensure they are coated evenly. Allow the fish to marinate for about 10 minutes.
3. While the fish is marinating, prepare the vegetables by slicing the bell peppers and red onion.
4. Place the marinated fish fillets, sliced bell peppers, and red onion in the cooking basket of one zone.
5. Select the "AIR FRY" program. Set the temperature to 200°C and set the cooking time to 15 minutes. Press START/STOP to begin cooking.
6. While the fish and vegetables are cooking, warm the flour tortillas according to package instructions or your preference.
7. Once the fish and vegetables are cooked, carefully remove them from the air fryer and let them cool for a few minutes. Flake the fish into smaller pieces.
8. Assemble the tacos by placing a generous amount of shredded lettuce, flaked fish, sliced bell peppers, and red onion on each tortilla.
9. Garnish with fresh cilantro leaves and serve with lime wedges on the side.
10. Enjoy your delicious **Fish and Vegetable Tacos**!

PORK STUFFING MEATBALLS | MAKES 30 MEATBALLS

Prep time: 10 min | Cook time: 10 min

- 500g ground pork
- 150g breadcrumbs
- 1 small onion, finely chopped
- 2 cloves of garlic, minced
- 2 tablespoons fresh parsley, chopped
- 1 tablespoon fresh sage, chopped
- 1 tablespoon fresh thyme, chopped
- 1 teaspoon salt
- 1/2 teaspoon black pepper
- 2 large eggs, beaten
- 30g butter, melted

DIRECTIONS:

1. In a large mixing bowl, combine the pork mince, breadcrumbs, chopped onion, minced garlic, chopped parsley, chopped sage, chopped thyme, salt, and black pepper. Mix well.
2. Add the beaten eggs to the mixture and mix until everything is evenly combined.
3. Shape the mixture into small meatballs, about the size of a golf ball, and place them on a baking sheet or tray lined with parchment paper. Evenly dividing them between the two zone.
4. Insert the baking sheet with the meatballs into both zone of the Air Fryer and close the lid.
5. Select zone 1, select AIR FRY and set temperature to 180°C and set time to 15 minutes. Select MATCH to duplicate settings across both zones. Press the START/STOP button to begin cooking.
6. While the meatballs are cooking, melt the butter in a small saucepan or microwave-safe dish.
7. When the meatballs are cooked, remove them from the Air Fryer and brush them with the melted butter for added flavor and moisture.
8. Serve the **pork stuffing meatballs** hot as an appetizer or main dish. They can be enjoyed on their own or served with a side of cranberry sauce or gravy.

COCONUT CHICKEN TENDERS | SERVES 4

Prep time: 15 min | Cook time: 12 min

- 500g chicken tenders
- 100g shredded coconut
- 50g breadcrumbs
- 2 eggs, beaten
- 30g all-purpose flour
- 1/2 teaspoon salt
- 1/2 teaspoon paprika
- Cooking spray

DIRECTIONS:

1. In a shallow bowl, combine the shredded coconut, breadcrumbs, salt, and paprika.
2. Place the flour in a separate shallow bowl.
3. Dip each chicken tender into the flour, shaking off any excess.
4. Dip the floured chicken tender into the beaten eggs, allowing any excess to drip off.
5. Roll the chicken tender in the coconut mixture, pressing gently to adhere the coating.
6. Repeat the process for the remaining chicken tenders.
7. Lightly coat the air fryer basket of both zone with cooking spray. Evenly dividing coated chicken tenders between the two zone. Place a single layer in each zone.
8. Select Zone 1, choose AIR FRY, set the temperature to 180°C, and set the time to 14 minutes. Select MATCH to duplicate settings across both zones. Press the START/STOP button to begin cooking.
9. Check the basket while cooking and gently shake the basket to make sure the food is cooks evenly.
10. Serve the **coconut chicken tenders** hot with your favorite dipping sauce.

<u>Note:</u> The cooking time may vary depending on the thickness of the chicken tenders. Adjust the cooking time as needed.

STEAK AND VEGETABLE KEBABS | SERVES 4

Prep time: 25 min | Cook time: 15 min

- 500g sirloin steak, cut into 2cm cubes
- 1 red bell pepper, seeded and cut into chunks
- 1 green bell pepper, seeded and cut into chunks
- 1 red onion, cut into chunks
- 8 cherry tomatoes
- 2 tablespoons olive oil
- 2 cloves garlic, minced
- 1 tablespoon Worcestershire sauce
- 1 tablespoon balsamic vinegar
- 1 teaspoon dried oregano
- Salt and pepper to taste
- Wooden or metal skewers

DIRECTIONS:

1. In a bowl, combine the olive oil, minced garlic, Worcestershire sauce, balsamic vinegar, dried oregano, salt, and pepper.
2. Add the cubed steak to the marinade and toss to coat. Let it marinate for 10 minutes.
3. Thread the marinated steak, bell peppers, red onion, and cherry tomatoes onto skewers, alternating between the ingredients.
4. Lightly coat the air fryer basket of both zone with cooking spray.
5. Evenly dividing and Place the kebabs in a single layer in each zone.
6. Select Zone 1, choose the AIR FRY program, set the temperature to 200°C, and set the time to 12-15 minutes for medium-rare to medium doneness, or adjust the cooking time based on your desired level of doneness. Select MATCH to duplicate settings across both zones. Press the START/STOP button to begin cooking.
7. Serve the **steak and vegetable kebabs** hot with your favorite dipping sauce or alongside a fresh salad.

FRIED GREEN TOMATOES
| SERVES 4

Prep time: 15 min | Cook time: 15 min

- 4 green tomatoes, sliced into 6mm thick rounds
- 120g all-purpose flour
- 1 teaspoon paprika
- 1/2 teaspoon garlic powder
- 1/2 teaspoon onion powder
- 1/4 teaspoon cayenne pepper (optional, for a spicy kick)
- Salt and pepper to taste
- 2 large eggs, beaten
- 80g breadcrumbs
- Cooking spray

DIRECTIONS:

1. In a shallow dish, combine the all-purpose flour, paprika, garlic powder, onion powder, cayenne pepper (if using), salt, and pepper. Mix well.
2. In another shallow dish, place the beaten eggs.
3. Place the breadcrumbs in a third shallow dish.
4. Dip each tomato slice into the flour mixture, coating both sides. Shake off any excess flour.
5. Dip the floured tomato slice into the beaten eggs, ensuring both sides are coated.
6. Finally, dip the tomato slice into the breadcrumbs, pressing gently to adhere the crumbs to the tomato.
7. Repeat the breading process for the remaining tomato slices.
8. Lightly coat the air fryer basket of both zone with cooking spray.
9. Place the breaded tomato slices in a single layer in two zone of the air fryer.
10. Select Zone 1, choose AIR FRY, set the temperature to 200°C, and set the time to 15 minutes. Select MATCH to duplicate settings across both zones. Press the START/STOP button to begin cooking.
11. Serve the **fried green tomatoes** hot as an appetizer or side dish. They are delicious on their own or served with a dipping sauce of your choice.

CHINESE-INSPIRED SPARERIBS
| SERVES 4

Prep time: 150 min | Cook time: 15 min

- 800g pork spareribs
- 2 tablespoons soy sauce
- 2 tablespoons hoisin sauce
- 2 tablespoons honey
- 1 tablespoon rice vinegar
- 2 cloves garlic, minced
- 1 teaspoon ginger, grated
- 1/2 teaspoon Chinese five-spice powder
- 1/4 teaspoon black pepper
- Optional garnish: chopped spring onions

DIRECTIONS:

1. In a bowl, combine the soy sauce, hoisin sauce, honey, rice vinegar, minced garlic, grated ginger, Chinese five-spice powder, and black pepper. Mix well to make the marinade.
2. Place the spareribs in a large ziplock bag or a shallow dish and pour the marinade over them. Ensure the ribs are well coated. Marinate for at least 2 hours or overnight in the refrigerator for best results.
3. Lightly coat the air fryer basket of both zone with cooking spray.
4. Evenly dividing the marinated spareribs between the two zone. Place them in a single layer in both zone of the air fryer, reserving any leftover marinade.
5. Select Zone 1, choose the AIR FRY program, set the temperature to 180°C, and set the time to 28 minutes. Select MATCH. Press the START/STOP.
6. While the spareribs are cooking, pour the reserved marinade into a small saucepan and bring it to a simmer. Let it cook for a few minutes until it thickens slightly, stirring occasionally. This will be used as a glaze for the cooked spareribs.
7. After the cooking time, carefully remove the spareribs and brush them with the glaze on both sides.
8. Once all the spareribs are cooked and glazed, garnish them with chopped spring onions if desired.
9. Serve the **Chinese-inspired spareribs** hot as a main dish. They can be enjoyed on their own or served with steamed rice and stir-fried vegetables.

PORK BURGERS WITH RED CABBAGE SALAD | SERVES 4

Prep time: 15 min | Cook time: 15 min

For the Pork Burgers:

- 500g minced pork
- 1 small onion, finely chopped
- 2 garlic cloves, minced
- 1 teaspoon dried sage
- 1 teaspoon dried thyme
- 1/2 teaspoon salt
- 1/4 teaspoon black pepper
- 4 burger buns
- Optional toppings: lettuce, tomato slices, sliced cheese, mayonnaise

For the Red Cabbage Salad:

- 200g red cabbage, finely shredded
- 1 small carrot, grated
- 2 tablespoons mayonnaise
- 1 tablespoon apple cider vinegar
- 1/2 teaspoon sugar
- Salt and pepper to taste

DIRECTIONS

1. In a bowl, combine the minced pork, chopped onion, minced garlic, dried sage, dried thyme, salt, and black pepper. Mix well to incorporate all the ingredients.
2. Divide the mixture into 4 equal portions and shape each portion into a patty.
3. Lightly coat the air fryer basket of both zone with cooking spray.
4. Evenly dividing the pork patty between the two zone.
5. Select Zone 1, choose the AIR FRY program, set the temperature to 200°C, and set the time to 15 minutes. Select MATCH to duplicate settings across both zones. Press the START/STOP button to begin cooking.
6. **Prepare the red cabbage salad:** In a separate bowl, combine the finely shredded red cabbage, grated carrot, mayonnaise, apple cider vinegar, sugar, salt, and pepper. Toss well to coat the vegetables in the dressing.
7. Toast the burger buns if desired.
8. Assemble the burgers by placing a cooked pork patty on each bun. Add desired toppings such as lettuce, tomato slices, sliced cheese, and mayonnaise.
9. Serve the **pork burgers with the red cabbage salad** on the side.
10. Enjoy the delicious and flavorful pork burgers with a refreshing and crunchy red cabbage salad.

Chapter 4: Fast & Easy Everyday Favourites

AIR FRIED BROCCOLI | SERVES 1

Prep time: 5 min | Cook time: 10 min

- 200g broccoli florets
- 1 tablespoon olive oil
- 1/2 teaspoon garlic powder
- 1/2 teaspoon paprika
- Salt and pepper to taste
- Lemon wedges, for serving (optional)

DIRECTIONS:

1. In a bowl, toss the broccoli florets with olive oil, garlic powder, paprika, salt, and pepper. Ensure the florets are evenly coated.
2. Place the seasoned broccoli florets in Zone 1 of the air fryer basket. Select the AIR FRY program. Set the temperature to 180°C. Set the cooking time to 12 minutes. Press START/STOP to begin cooking.
3. While the broccoli is cooking, you can prepare any additional dishes or sides.
4. Once the cooking time is complete, remove the air fryer basket from Zone 1 and transfer the air-fried broccoli to a serving plate.
5. Serve the **air-fried broccoli** hot, optionally with a squeeze of fresh lemon juice for added flavor.

SCALLOPED VEGGIE MIX | SERVES 4

Prep time: 15 min | Cook time: 25 min

- 500g mixed vegetables (such as carrots, broccoli, cauliflower)
- 1 tablespoon butter
- 1 tablespoon all-purpose flour
- 250ml milk
- 100g grated cheese (such as cheddar or Gruyere)
- 1/2 teaspoon garlic powder
- Salt and pepper to taste
- Fresh parsley, chopped (for garnish)

DIRECTIONS:

1. In a pot of boiling water, cook the mixed vegetables until they are slightly tender. Drain and set aside.
2. In a separate saucepan, melt the butter over medium heat. Stir in the flour and cook for 1-2 minutes until it forms a paste.
3. Gradually whisk in the milk until the mixture becomes smooth and thickens. Cook for an additional 2-3 minutes, stirring constantly.
4. Remove the saucepan from the heat and stir in the grated cheese until it melts and forms a creamy sauce. Season with garlic powder, salt, and pepper.
5. In Zone 1 of the air fryer basket, layer half of the cooked vegetables. Pour half of the cheese sauce over the vegetables.
6. Repeat the layering process with the remaining vegetables and cheese sauce in Zone 2.
7. Select zone 1, select BAKE and set temperature to 180°C and set time to 25 minutes. Select MATCH to duplicate settings across both zones. Press the START/STOP button to begin cooking.
8. Once the cooking time is complete, remove the air fryer basket and let it cool for a few minutes.
9. Garnish with fresh chopped parsley and serve the **Scalloped Veggie Mix** hot.

CHEESY BAKED GRITS | SERVES 6

Prep time: 10 min | Cook time: 30 min

- 160g grits
- 950ml water
- 1 teaspoon salt
- 200g grated cheddar cheese
- 30g grated Parmesan cheese
- 30g butter
- 120ml milk
- 2 large eggs, beaten
- 1/2 teaspoon garlic powder
- Salt and pepper to taste
- Chopped fresh parsley (for garnish)

DIRECTIONS:

1. In a saucepan, bring the water to a boil. Add the salt and slowly whisk in the grits. Reduce the heat to low and simmer for about 5 minutes, stirring occasionally, until the grits are thickened.
2. Stir in the grated cheddar cheese, Parmesan cheese, butter, milk, garlic powder, salt, and pepper into the cooked grits until the cheese is melted and the mixture is well combined.
3. Remove the saucepan from the heat and let it cool for a few minutes. Stir in the beaten eggs until fully incorporated.
4. In Zone 1 of the air fryer basket, pour the cheesy grits mixture. Place the basket in the Air Fryer.
5. Select Zone 1, then choosing the BAKE program and setting the temperature to 180°C in 30 minutes until the top is golden and the edges are slightly crisp.
6. Once the cooking time is complete, remove the air fryer basket and let it cool for a few minutes.
7. Garnish with chopped fresh parsley and serve the **Cheesy Baked Grits** hot.

BEERY AND CRUNCHY ONION RINGS | SERVES 2 TO 4

Prep time: 15 min | Cook time: 10 min

- 2 large onions
- 200g all-purpose flour
- 1 teaspoon paprika
- 1/2 teaspoon garlic powder
- 1/2 teaspoon salt
- 1/4 teaspoon black pepper
- 250ml beer (preferably a light lager)
- Vegetable oil, for frying
- Dipping sauce of your choice (e.g., ketchup, mayo, BBQ sauce)

DIRECTIONS:

1. Peel the onions and slice them into thick rings. Separate the rings and set them aside.
2. In a mixing bowl, combine the flour, paprika, garlic powder, salt, and black pepper. Whisk until well combined.
3. Gradually pour the beer into the flour mixture, whisking continuously, until you have a smooth batter with a thick consistency.
4. Dip each onion ring into the batter, ensuring it is fully coated, and then let any excess batter drip off.
5. Place the coated onion rings in a single layer in both Zone of air Fryer.
6. Select zone 1, select AIR FRY and set temperature to 200°C and set time to 10 minutes. Select MATCH to duplicate settings across both zones. Press the START/STOP button to begin cooking.
7. Near the end of the cooking time, check the onions for golden brown and crispy. If not, cook for another 3-5 minutes.
8. Once the onion rings are cooked, remove them from the air fryer and transfer to a paper towel-lined plate to drain any excess oil.
9. Serve the **Beery and Crunchy Onion Rings** hot with your favorite dipping sauce.

AIR FRIED COURGETTE STICKS | SERVES 4

Prep time: 15 min | Cook time: 10 min

- 2 medium courgettes (zucchini)
- 100g breadcrumbs
- 50g grated Parmesan cheese
- 1 teaspoon dried mixed herbs
- 1/2 teaspoon garlic powder
- 1/2 teaspoon salt
- 1/4 teaspoon black pepper
- 2 large eggs, beaten
- Cooking spray or olive oil, for greasing

DIRECTIONS:

1. Wash the courgettes and cut them into sticks, approximately 1 cm thick and 7-8 cm long. Set aside.
2. In a shallow dish, combine the breadcrumbs, grated Parmesan cheese, dried mixed herbs, garlic powder, salt, and black pepper. Mix well.
3. Dip each courgette stick into the beaten eggs, allowing any excess to drip off.
4. Roll the egg-coated courgette stick in the breadcrumb mixture, pressing lightly to ensure it is evenly coated. Repeat with the remaining courgette sticks.
5. Lightly grease the air fryer basket with cooking spray or a small amount of olive oil to prevent sticking.
6. In Zone 1 of the air fryer basket, place the coated courgette sticks in a single layer. You may need to cook them in two zone depending on the size of your air fryer.
7. Select Zone 1, choosing AIR FRY and setting the temperature to 200°C in10 minutes. Check them until the courgette sticks are golden brown and crispy.
8. Once the courgette sticks are cooked, remove them from the air fryer and transfer to a serving plate
9. Serve the **Air Fried Courgette Sticks** hot as a delicious appetizer or side dish. They can be enjoyed on their own or with a dipping sauce of your choice, such as marinara sauce or tzatziki.

SIMPLE AND EASY CROUTONS | SERVES 4

Prep time: 5 min | Cook time: 7 min

- 4 slices of bread (white or wholemeal)
- 2 tablespoons olive oil
- 1 teaspoon dried herbs (such as thyme, oregano, or Italian seasoning)
- 1/2 teaspoon garlic powder (optional)
- Salt and pepper to taste.

DIRECTIONS:

1. Cut the bread slices into small cubes or bite-sized pieces.
2. In a bowl, combine the olive oil, dried herbs, salt, and pepper. Mix well.
3. Add the bread cubes to the bowl and toss them gently to coat them evenly with the seasoned oil mixture.
4. Place the seasoned bread cubes in Zone 1 of the air fryer basket, ensuring they are in a single layer for even cooking.
5. Insert the air fryer basket into air fryer zone 1. Select Zone 1, choosing AIR FRY, set the temperature to 180°C, set the cooking time to 7 minutes. Keep an eye on the croutons and shake the basket or stir them occasionally for even browning. Check them periodically to avoid burning.
6. Once the croutons are done, remove them from the air fryer and let them cool slightly before using or storing.
7. Serve the **Simple and Easy Croutons** as a crunchy topping for salads, soups, or as a delicious snack on their own.

TRADITIONAL QUESO FUNDIDO | SERVES 4

Prep time: 10 min | Cook time: 10 min

- 200g grated Cheddar cheese
- 200g grated Monterey Jack cheese
- 1 tablespoon olive oil
- 1 small onion, finely chopped
- 2 cloves garlic, minced
- 1 jalapeno pepper, seeded and finely chopped (optional)
- 1/2 teaspoon ground cumin
- 1/2 teaspoon paprika
- Salt and pepper, to taste
- Tortilla chips, for serving

DIRECTIONS:

1. In a skillet, heat the vegetable oil over medium heat. Add the diced onion and jalapeño pepper (if using) and sauté until softened, about 3-4 minutes. Add the minced garlic to the skillet and sauté for an additional minute.
2. Add the diced tomatoes to the skillet and cook for 2-3 minutes, stirring occasionally, until the tomatoes are heated through.
3. In Zone 1, place the grated Cheddar cheese and Monterey Jack cheese in an even layer.
4. Insert the air fryer basket into Air Fryer. Select Zone 1, choosing AIR FRY and setting the temperature to 180°C in 5 minutes. This will melt the cheese and create a gooey base.
5. After 5 minutes, carefully remove the air fryer basket and top the melted cheese with the sautéed onion, jalapeño, garlic, and diced tomatoes.
6. Return the air fryer basket to Zone 1 of the air fryer and continue cooking for an additional 5 minutes or until the cheese is fully melted and bubbling.
7. Once done, remove the air fryer basket from the Ninja Dual Zone Air Fryer and sprinkle the chopped fresh cilantro over the melted cheese.
8. Season with salt and pepper to taste.
9. Serve the **Traditional Queso Fundido** immediately with tortilla chips for dipping.

BEETROOT SALAD WITH LEMON VINAIGRETTE | SERVES 4

Prep time: 15 min | Cook time: 20 min

- 4 medium beetroots, peeled and sliced
- 100g mixed salad greens
- 50g crumbled feta cheese
- 2 tablespoons chopped fresh parsley

For the Lemon Vinaigrette:
- 2 tablespoons freshly squeezed lemon juice
- 4 tablespoons extra virgin olive oil
- 1 teaspoon Dijon mustard
- Salt and pepper to taste

DIRECTIONS:

1. In Zone 1 of the air fryer basket, place the sliced beetroots in a single layer. You may need to cook them in two zone depending on the size of your air fryer.
2. Select Zone 1, choose the AIR FRY, temperature :180°C in 15-20 minutes or until they are tender when pierced with a fork. (Select MACTH if cook in both zone)
3. While the beetroots are cooking, prepare the lemon vinaigrette. In a small bowl, whisk together the lemon juice, olive oil, Dijon mustard, salt, and pepper until well combined. Set aside.
4. Once the beetroots are cooked, remove the air fryer basket from Zone 1 and let the beetroots cool for a few minutes.
5. In a large bowl, combine the mixed salad greens and the air-fried beetroot slices. Drizzle the lemon vinaigrette over the salad and toss gently to coat.
6. Sprinkle the crumbled feta cheese and chopped fresh parsley over the salad.
7. Serve the **Beetroot Salad with Lemon Vinaigrette** immediately as a refreshing and vibrant side dish.

PURPLE POTATO CHIPS WITH ROSEMARY | SERVES 6

Prep time: 10 min | Cook time: 15 min

- 500g purple potatoes
- 2 tablespoons olive oil
- 1 tablespoon chopped fresh rosemary
- Salt to taste

DIRECTIONS:

1. Wash and scrub the purple potatoes thoroughly to remove any dirt. Leave the skin on for added color and texture. Slice the potatoes into thin, even rounds using a mandoline or a sharp knife.
2. In a large bowl, toss the potato slices with olive oil, chopped fresh rosemary, and salt. Make sure each slice is well coated with the oil and seasoning.
3. Place a single layer of the seasoned potato slices in both zone of the air fryer. Select zone 1, select AIR FRY and set temperature to 180°C and set time to 15 minutes. Select MATCH to duplicate settings across both zones. Press the START/STOP button to begin cooking.
4. Once the cooking time is complete, remove the basket from the Air Fryer and let the chips cool for a few minutes. They will continue to crisp up as they cool down.
5. Serve the **Purple Potato Chips with Rosemary** as a tasty and colorful snack or as a side dish to complement your meals.

BAKED CHEESE SANDWICH | SERVES 2

Prep time: 10 min | Cook time: 10 min

- 4 slices of bread (white, whole wheat, or your preferred choice)
- Butter, softened, for spreading
- 100g cheddar cheese, grated
- 50g mozzarella cheese, grated
- 2 tablespoons mayonnaise
- 1 teaspoon Dijon mustard
- Salt and pepper to taste
- Optional toppings: sliced tomatoes, cooked bacon, ham, or any other desired fillings

DIRECTIONS:

1. In a small bowl, mix together the grated cheddar cheese and mozzarella cheese.
2. In another bowl, combine the mayonnaise and Dijon mustard. Season with salt and pepper to taste.
3. Spread butter on one side of each bread slice. Place two slices, buttered side down, in Zone 1 of the air fryer basket.
4. Spread the mayonnaise and mustard mixture evenly on the non-buttered side of the bread slices.
5. Sprinkle the cheese mixture on top of the mayonnaise-mustard mixture. Add any desired toppings, such as sliced tomatoes, cooked bacon, or ham.
6. Place the remaining two slices of bread on top, buttered side up. Then place them in basket of zone 1.
7. Select zone 1, select BAKE, set temperature to 180°C and set time to 10 minutes. Press the START/STOP button to begin cooking.
8. After 5 minutes, carefully flip the sandwich using a spatula or tongs to ensure even browning on both sides.
9. Continue cooking for the remaining 5 minutes or until the bread turns golden brown and the cheese is melted and gooey.
10. Once cooked, remove the **Baked Cheese Sandwich** from the Ninja Dual Zone Air Fryer and let it cool for a few minutes before slicing and serving.
11. Serve the Baked Cheese Sandwich as a delicious and satisfying meal or snack.

INDIAN-STYLE SWEET POTATO FRIES | MAKES 20 FRIES

Prep time: 10 min | Cook time: 10 min

- 2 large sweet potatoes
- 2 tablespoons olive oil
- 1 teaspoon ground cumin
- 1 teaspoon ground coriander
- 1/2 teaspoon ground turmeric
- 1/2 teaspoon paprika
- 1/2 teaspoon salt
- Freshly ground black pepper to taste
- Chopped fresh coriander (cilantro), for garnish (optional)
- Lime wedges, for serving

DIRECTIONS:

1. Wash and peel the sweet potatoes. Cut them into thin, even-sized fries.
2. In a bowl, combine the olive oil, ground cumin, ground coriander, ground turmeric, paprika, salt, and black pepper. Mix well to form a spice mixture.
3. Place the sweet potato fries in a large bowl and drizzle the spice mixture over them. Toss until the fries are evenly coated with the spices.
4. Divide the sweet potato fries evenly between Zones 1 and 2 of the air fryer basket. Spread them out in a single layer for even cooking.
5. Select zone 1, select AIR FRY and set temperature to 200°C and set time to 15 minutes. Select MATCH to duplicate settings across both zones. Press the START/STOP button to begin cooking.
6. After 10 minutes, carefully remove the basket and shake it to ensure even cooking. Return the basket to the air fryer and continue cooking for the remaining 5 minutes or until the fries are crispy and golden brown.
7. Once cooked, remove the **Indian-Style Sweet Potato Fries** from the Air Fryer and transfer them to a serving dish.
8. Garnish with chopped fresh coriander (cilantro), if desired, and serve hot with lime wedges on the side for added zest.

BACON PINWHEELS | MAKES 8 PINWHEELS

Prep time: 10 min | Cook time: 15 min

- 1 sheet ready-made puff pastry
- 8 slices streaky bacon
- 100 grams grated Cheddar cheese
- 1 tablespoon Dijon mustard
- Freshly ground black pepper, to taste
- Chopped fresh parsley, for garnish (optional)

DIRECTIONS:

1. Lay out the sheet of puff pastry on a clean surface. Spread the Dijon mustard evenly over the puff pastry.
2. Sprinkle the grated Cheddar cheese over the mustard, making sure to cover the entire surface of the puff pastry.
3. Season with freshly ground black pepper to taste.
4. Starting from one end, tightly roll up the puff pastry into a log shape.
5. Cut the rolled puff pastry log into 8 equal-sized slices.
6. Take a slice of streaky bacon and wrap it around one of the puff pastry slices, ensuring the bacon covers the entire slice.
7. Repeat the process for the remaining puff pastry slices and bacon.
8. Place the bacon-wrapped puff pastry pinwheels in both zone1 of the air fryer basket, making sure they are spaced apart.
9. Select zone 1, select AIR FRY and set temperature to 200°C and set time to 15 minutes. Select MATCH to duplicate settings across both zones. Press the START/STOP button to begin cooking.
10. After 10 minutes, carefully remove the basket and flip the bacon pinwheels to ensure even cooking. Return the basket to the air fryer and continue cooking for the remaining 5 minutes or until the bacon is crispy and the puff pastry is golden brown.
11. Once cooked, remove the **Bacon Pinwheels** from the Air Fryer and transfer them to a serving dish.
12. Garnish with chopped fresh parsley, if desired, serve hot as a delicious appetizer or snack.

BRUSCHETTA CHICKEN | SERVES 4

Prep time: 15 min | Cook time: 20 min

- 4 boneless, skinless chicken breasts
- 2 tablespoons olive oil
- 2 cloves garlic, minced
- 1 teaspoon dried basil
- 1 teaspoon dried oregano
- Salt and pepper to taste
- 4 slices mozzarella cheese
- 4 large tomato slices
- Fresh basil leaves, for garnish

For the Bruschetta Topping:

- 2 large tomatoes, diced
- 2 cloves garlic, minced
- 2 tablespoons extra-virgin olive oil
- 1 tablespoon balsamic vinegar
- 1 tablespoon fresh basil, chopped
- Salt and pepper to taste

DIRECTIONS

1. In a bowl, combine the diced tomatoes, minced garlic, olive oil, balsamic vinegar, fresh basil, salt, and pepper. Mix well to make the bruschetta topping. Set aside.
2. Place the chicken breasts on a clean surface and drizzle them with olive oil. Rub the minced garlic, dried basil, dried oregano, salt, and pepper onto both sides of the chicken.
3. Insert the crisper plates back into the drawers of the air fryer. Place 2 chicken breasts in each drawer, ensuring they are evenly spaced.
4. In Zone 1, select the AIR FRY function, set the temperature to 200°C, and set the time to 15 minutes. Press the MATCH. Press the START/STOP to begin cooking.
5. While the chicken cooks, prepare the tomato slices and mozzarella cheese.
6. After 10 minutes of cooking, open the drawers and place a slice of mozzarella cheese on each chicken breast. Close the drawers and continue cooking.
7. Once the cooking time is complete, remove the chicken from the air fryer and let it rest for a few minutes.
8. Meanwhile, lightly toast the slices of bread by place them on the crisper plates in 1 zone, select ROAST, temperature to 180°C and the time to 2 minutes.
9. Place a tomato slice on top of each chicken breast, followed by a spoonful of the bruschetta topping.
10. Garnish with fresh basil leaves and serve the **Bruschetta Chicken** with toasted bread slices.

GOLDEN CHICKEN CUTLETS | SERVES 4

Prep time: 15 min | Cook time: 12 min

- 4 boneless, skinless chicken breasts
- 240g breadcrumbs
- 2 teaspoons paprika
- 1 teaspoon garlic powder
- 1 teaspoon dried thyme
- 1 teaspoon dried parsley
- Salt and pepper to taste
- 2 large eggs
- Cooking spray

For the Lemon-Herb Sauce:

- 120g mayonnaise
- 1 tablespoon lemon juice
- 1 teaspoon Dijon mustard
- 1 tablespoon fresh parsley, chopped
- 1 tablespoon fresh dill, chopped
- Salt and pepper to taste

DIRECTIONS

1. In a shallow dish, combine the breadcrumbs, paprika, garlic powder, dried thyme, dried parsley, salt, and pepper. Mix well.
2. In another shallow dish, whisk the eggs until well beaten.
3. Dip each chicken breast into the beaten eggs, allowing any excess to drip off, then coat it with the breadcrumb mixture. Press the breadcrumbs onto the chicken to ensure they adhere well.
4. Insert the crisper plates back into the drawers of the air fryer. Place 2 chicken breasts in each drawer, ensuring they are evenly spaced.
5. In Zone 1, select the AIR FRY function, set the temperature to 200°C, and set the time to 10 minutes.
6. Press the MATCH. Press the START/STOP button to begin cooking.
7. After 6 minutes of cooking, open the drawers and lightly spray the chicken cutlets with cooking spray to promote browning.
8. Close the drawers and continue cooking for the remaining time.
9. While the chicken cooks, prepare the lemon-herb sauce. In a bowl, combine the mayonnaise, lemon juice, Dijon mustard, fresh parsley, fresh dill, salt, and pepper. Mix well.
10. Once the cooking time is complete, remove the chicken cutlets from the air fryer and let them rest for a few minutes.
11. Serve the **Golden Chicken Cutlets** with the lemon-herb sauce on the side.

SPICE-RUBBED CHICKEN THIGHS | SERVES 4

Prep time: 10 min | Cook time: 20 min

- 8 bone-in, skin-on chicken thighs
- 1 tablespoon paprika
- 1 teaspoon ground cumin
- 1 teaspoon ground coriander
- 1 teaspoon garlic powder
- 1 teaspoon onion powder
- 1/2 teaspoon cayenne pepper (adjust according to spice preference)
- 1 teaspoon salt
- 1/2 teaspoon black pepper
- Cooking spray

DIRECTIONS:

1. In a small bowl, combine the paprika, ground cumin, ground coriander, garlic powder, onion powder, cayenne pepper, salt, and black pepper. Mix well to create the spice rub.
2. Pat dry the chicken thighs with a paper towel and place them on a clean surface.
3. Sprinkle the spice rub evenly over both sides of the chicken thighs, pressing gently to adhere the spices.
4. Insert the crisper plates back into the drawers of the air fryer. Place 4 chicken thighs in each drawer, ensuring they are evenly spaced.
5. In Zone 1, select the AIR FRY function, set the temperature to 200°C, and set the time to 20 minutes. Press the MATCH. Press the START/STOP to begin cooking.
6. After 10 minutes of cooking, open the drawers and lightly spray the chicken thighs with cooking spray to promote browning.
7. Close the drawers and continue cooking for the remaining time.
8. Once the cooking time is complete, remove the chicken thighs from the air fryer and let them rest for a few minutes.
9. Serve the **Spice-Rubbed Chicken Thighs** as desired, such as with a side salad or roasted vegetables.

PICKLE BRINED FRIED CHICKEN | SERVES 4

Prep time: 15 min | Cook time: 25 min

For the Brine:
- 240 ml dill pickle juice
- 240 ml buttermilk
- 4 bone-in, skin-on chicken pieces (such as drumsticks or thighs)

For the Coating:
- 120 grams all-purpose flour
- 1 teaspoon paprika
- 1 teaspoon garlic powder
- 1 teaspoon onion powder
- 1/2 teaspoon salt
- 1/4 teaspoon black pepper
- Cooking spray

DIRECTIONS:

1. In a large bowl, combine the dill pickle juice and buttermilk to create the brine.
2. Add the chicken pieces to the brine, making sure they are fully submerged. Cover the bowl and refrigerate for 1-2 hours to allow the chicken to brine.
3. In a shallow dish, combine the all-purpose flour, paprika, garlic powder, onion powder, salt, and black pepper. Mix well.
4. Remove each chicken piece from the brine, allowing any excess liquid to drip off, and coat it in the flour mixture, pressing gently to ensure the coating adheres.
5. Insert the crisper plate back into the drawers of the air fryer. Place 4 chicken pieces in Zone 1. Select the AIR FRY, set temperature to 200°C in 20 minutes. Press the START/STOP.
6. After 15 minutes of cooking, open the drawer and lightly spray the chicken pieces with cooking spray to promote browning.
7. Close the drawer and continue cooking for the remaining time.
8. Once the cooking time is complete, remove the chicken pieces from the air fryer and let them rest for a few minutes.
9. Serve the **Pickle Brined Fried Chicken** hot with your choice of sides and dipping sauces.

AFRICAN MERGUEZ MEATBALLS I SERVES 4

Prep time: 15 min | Cook time: 12 min

- 500g ground poultry (such as chicken or turkey)
- 1 small onion, finely chopped
- 2 garlic cloves, minced
- 1 teaspoon ground cumin
- 1 teaspoon ground coriander
- 1 teaspoon paprika
- 1/2 teaspoon ground cinnamon
- 1/2 teaspoon cayenne pepper (adjust to taste)
- 1/2 teaspoon salt
- 1/4 teaspoon black pepper
- 2 tablespoons chopped fresh parsley
- 2 tablespoons chopped fresh cilantro
- 1 tablespoon olive oil

DIRECTIONS

1. In a large bowl, combine the ground poultry, chopped onion, minced garlic, ground cumin, ground coriander, paprika, ground cinnamon, cayenne pepper, salt, black pepper, chopped parsley, and chopped cilantro. Mix well until all the ingredients are evenly incorporated.
2. Shape the mixture into small meatballs, about 1-2 inches in diameter.
3. In Zone 1, place the meatballs in a single layer on the crisper plates, ensuring they are not touching each other.select the AIR FRY function. Set the temperature to 180°C and the time to 12 minutes.
4. Drizzle the olive oil over the meatballs to help them brown and prevent sticking.
5. Press the START/STOP button to begin cooking.
6. After 5-6 minutes, open the drawer in Zone 1 and gently shake it to rotate the meatballs.
7. Close the drawer and continue cooking for another 5-6 minutes or until the meatballs are cooked through and nicely browned.
8. Once done, remove the **meatballs** from the air fryer and let them rest for a few minutes before serving.

HONEY-GLAZED CHICKEN THIGHS I SERVES 4

Prep time: 40 min | Cook time: 25 min

- 8 chicken thighs, bone-in and skin-on
- 2 tablespoons olive oil
- 2 tablespoons honey
- 2 tablespoons soy sauce
- 2 cloves garlic, minced
- 1 teaspoon ground paprika
- 1/2 teaspoon dried thyme
- Salt and pepper to taste
- Fresh parsley, chopped (for garnish)

DIRECTIONS

1. In a large bowl, whisk together the olive oil, honey, soy sauce, minced garlic, ground paprika, dried thyme, salt, and pepper to create the marinade.
2. Add the chicken thighs to the marinade, ensuring they are coated evenly. Cover the bowl and let the chicken marinate in the refrigerator for 30 minutes.
3. Once the chicken has marinated, remove it from the marinade, allowing any excess marinade to drip off.
4. Place 4 chicken thighs in each zone of the air fryer, making sure they are evenly spaced.
5. In Zone 1, select the AIR FRY function, set the temperature to 180°C, and set the time to 25 minutes.Press the MACTH. Press the START/STOP button to begin cooking.
6. After 15 minutes of cooking, open the drawers and brush the chicken thighs with any remaining marinade.
7. Close the drawers and continue cooking for the remaining time or until the chicken thighs are cooked through and golden brown.
8. Once the cooking time is complete, remove the chicken thighs from the air fryer and let them rest for a few minutes.
9. Garnish the **Honey-Glazed Chicken Thighs** with freshly chopped parsley.
10. Serve the chicken thighs hot with your choice of sides, such as roasted vegetables, rice, or salad.

CHICKEN, COURGETTE, AND SPINACH SALAD
I SERVES 4

Prep time: 15 min | Cook time: 15 min

For the Chicken:

- 4 boneless, skinless chicken breasts
- 1 tablespoon olive oil
- 1 teaspoon paprika
- 1/2 teaspoon garlic powder
- 1/2 teaspoon onion powder
- 1/2 teaspoon dried thyme
- Salt and pepper to taste

For the Salad:

- 2 medium courgettes (zucchini), thinly sliced
- 200 grams baby spinach leaves
- 200 grams cherry tomatoes, halved
- 1/2 red onion, thinly sliced
- 50 grams feta cheese, crumbled

For the Dressing:

- 3 tablespoons extra virgin olive oil
- 2 tablespoons lemon juice
- 1 teaspoon Dijon mustard
- 1 teaspoon honey
- Salt and pepper to taste

DIRECTIONS

1. In a small bowl, combine the paprika, garlic powder, onion powder, dried thyme, salt, and pepper to create the seasoning for the chicken.
2. Rub the chicken breasts with olive oil and then sprinkle the seasoning mixture evenly on both sides of each chicken breast.
3. Place the seasoned chicken breasts in Zone 1 of the air fryer.
4. In Zone 2, place the thinly sliced courgettes (zucchini) on the crisper plate.
5. In Zone 1, select the AIR FRY function, set the temperature to 200°C, and set the time to 15 minutes.
6. In Zone 2, select the AIR FRY function, set the temperature to 180°C, and set the time to 7 minutes.
7. (If like, Press the SYNC button to automatically sync the cook times of both zones) Press the START/STOP button to begin cooking.
8. After haft of cooking time, open the drawer in each zone and gently shake it.
9. While the chicken and courgettes are cooking, prepare the salad by combining the baby spinach leaves, cherry tomatoes, red onion, and crumbled feta cheese in a large bowl.
10. In a separate small bowl, whisk together the extra virgin olive oil, lemon juice, Dijon mustard, honey, salt, and pepper to create the dressing.
11. Once the cooking time is complete, remove the chicken breasts and courgettes from the air fryer.
12. Allow the chicken to rest for a few minutes, then slice it into thin strips.
13. Add the cooked courgettes and sliced chicken to the salad bowl.
14. Drizzle the dressing over the salad and toss well to coat all the ingredients.
15. Serve the **Chicken, Courgette, and Spinach Salad** immediately as a delicious and healthy meal.

EASY CHICKEN NACHOS | SERVES 8

Prep time: 10 min |Cook time: 10 min

- 400 grams tortilla chips
- 200 grams cooked chicken, shredded
- 100 grams grated cheddar cheese
- 100 grams grated mozzarella cheese
- 75 grams diced tomatoes
- 75 grams diced red onion
- 30 grams sliced jalapeños (optional)
- 15 grams chopped fresh coriander (cilantro)
- Sour cream and guacamole, for serving

DIRECTIONS:

1. In each zone, spread a layer of tortilla chips on the crisper plate, ensuring they are evenly distributed. Distribute half of the shredded chicken evenly over the tortilla chips.
2. Sprinkle both zones with a combination of cheddar and mozzarella cheese.
3. In Zone 1, select the AIR FRY function, set the temperature to 180°C, and set the time to 10 minutes. Press the MATCH. Press the START/STOP button to begin cooking.
4. While the nachos are cooking, prepare the toppings by dicing the tomatoes, red onion, and jalapeños (if using), and chopping the fresh coriander (cilantro).
5. Once the cooking time is complete, remove the drawers from the air fryer and let the nachos cool for a few minutes.
6. Sprinkle the diced tomatoes, red onion, jalapeños (if using), and fresh coriander evenly over both zones of the nachos.
7. Serve the **Easy Chicken Nachos** hot with sour cream and guacamole on the side.

TURKEY MEATLOAF | SERVES 4

Prep time: 15 min |Cook time: 30 min

- 500 grams ground turkey
- 60 grams breadcrumbs
- 40 grams finely chopped onion
- 40 grams finely chopped red bell pepper
- 40 grams grated carrot
- 60 ml milk
- 1 large egg, lightly beaten
- 2 tablespoons Worcestershire sauce
- 1 tablespoon tomato paste
- 1 teaspoon dried thyme
- 1 teaspoon dried oregano
- 1/2 teaspoon garlic powder
- 1/2 teaspoon salt
- 1/4 teaspoon black pepper
- 2 tablespoons ketchup (for topping)

DIRECTIONS:

1. In a large mixing bowl, combine the ground turkey, breadcrumbs, finely chopped onion, red bell pepper, grated carrot, milk, lightly beaten egg, Worcestershire sauce, tomato paste, dried thyme, dried oregano, garlic powder, salt, and black pepper. Mix well until all the ingredients are evenly incorporated.
2. Divide the meat mixture in half and shape each portion into a loaf shape.
3. In Zone 1, place one meatloaf in the center of the crisper plate.
4. In Zone 2, place the second meatloaf in the center of the crisper plate.
5. In Zone 1, select the AIR FRY function, set temperature to 180°C, and set the time to 30 minutes. Press the MATCH. Press the START/STOP button to begin cooking.
6. After 18 minutes of cooking, open the drawers and spread 1 tablespoon of ketchup evenly over the top of each meatloaf.
7. Close the drawers and continue cooking for the remaining time.
8. Once the cooking time is complete, remove the drawers from the air fryer and let the meatloaves rest for a few minutes.
9. Slice the **Turkey Meatloaf** into portions and serve hot.
10. Enjoy the flavorful Turkey Meatloaf with choice of sides, such as mashed potatoes and steamed vegetables.

STUFFED TURKEY ROULADE | SERVES 4

Prep time: 20 min | Cook time: 35 min

- 500 grams boneless turkey breast
- 100 grams fresh spinach leaves
- 50 grams feta cheese, crumbled
- 50 grams sun-dried tomatoes, chopped
- 25 grams pine nuts

- 1 tablespoon olive oil
- 1 teaspoon dried oregano
- 1/2 teaspoon garlic powder
- Salt and pepper, to taste

DIRECTIONS

1. Lay the boneless turkey breast flat on a cutting board and carefully butterfly it by making a horizontal cut through the center, taking care not to cut all the way through. Open up the turkey breast like a book.
2. In Zone 1, lay down a sheet of plastic wrap on the crisper plate. Place the butterflied turkey breast on the plastic wrap and cover it with another sheet of plastic wrap.
3. Use a meat mallet or rolling pin to flatten the turkey breast to an even thickness.
4. Remove the top sheet of plastic wrap. Season the turkey breast with dried oregano, garlic powder, salt, and pepper.
5. In Zone 2, heat the olive oil. Add the fresh spinach leaves, select the AIR FRY function, set the temperature to 180°C, and set the time to 4-5 minutes. Press the START/STOP.
6. Spread the wilted spinach evenly over the turkey breast.
7. Sprinkle the crumbled feta cheese, chopped sun-dried tomatoes, and pine nuts over the spinach layer.
8. Starting from one end, carefully roll up the turkey breast tightly, using the plastic wrap to help you.
9. Remove the plastic wrap from the rolled turkey roulade.
10. In Zone 1, select the AIR FRY function, set the temperature to 180°C, and set the time to 30-35 minutes. Press the START/STOP.
11. Once the cooking time is complete, remove the drawers from the air fryer and let the turkey roulade rest for a few minutes before slicing.
12. Slice the Stuffed Turkey Roulade into portions and serve hot.
13. Enjoy the flavorful **Stuffed Turkey Roulade** with your choice of sides, such as roasted vegetables and mashed potatoes.

BARBECUED CHICKEN WITH CREAMY COLESLAW I SERVES 2

Prep time: 15 min | Cook time: 25 min

For the Barbecued Chicken:

- 2 chicken breasts
- 4 tablespoons barbecue sauce
- 1 tablespoon olive oil
- 1 teaspoon smoked paprika
- 1/2 teaspoon garlic powder
- Salt and pepper, to taste

For the Creamy Coleslaw:

- 200 grams shredded cabbage
- 50 grams grated carrot
- 2 tablespoons mayonnaise
- 1 tablespoon Greek yogurt
- 1 tablespoon apple cider vinegar
- 1 teaspoon Dijon mustard
- 1 teaspoon honey
- Salt and pepper, to taste

DIRECTIONS

For the Barbecued Chicken:

1. In a bowl, combine the barbecue sauce, olive oil, smoked paprika, garlic powder, salt, and pepper. Mix well.
2. Place the chicken breasts in a shallow dish and pour half of the barbecue sauce mixture over them, reserving the remaining sauce for basting.
3. In Zone 1, place the chicken breasts on the crisper plate. Select the AIR FRY function, set the temperature to 180°C, and set the time to 20-25 minutes. Press the START/STOP button to begin cooking.
4. After 10 minutes of cooking, open the drawers and brush the chicken breasts with the reserved barbecue sauce mixture.
5. Close the drawer and continue cooking until the chicken is cooked through.
6. Once cooked, remove the chicken from the air fryer and let it rest for a few minutes before slicing.

For the Creamy Coleslaw:

1. In a large bowl, combine the shredded cabbage and grated carrot.
2. In a separate small bowl, whisk together the mayonnaise, Greek yogurt, apple cider vinegar, Dijon mustard, honey, salt, and pepper until well combined.
3. Pour the dressing over the cabbage and carrot mixture. Toss until the vegetables are well coated.
4. Adjust the seasoning according to your taste preferences.
5. Serve the barbecued chicken alongside the creamy coleslaw. It pairs well with additional barbecue sauce or a side of fries

EASY CAJUN CHICKEN DRUMSTICKS | SERVES 4

Prep time: 10 min | Cook time: 30 min

- 8 chicken drumsticks
- 2 tablespoons olive oil
- 1 tablespoon Cajun seasoning
- 1 teaspoon paprika
- 1 teaspoon garlic powder
- 1/2 teaspoon salt
- 1/4 teaspoon black pepper

DIRECTIONS:

1. In a bowl, combine the olive oil, Cajun seasoning, paprika, garlic powder, salt, and black pepper. Mix well to create a marinade.
2. Place the chicken drumsticks in a shallow dish and coat them with the marinade, ensuring they are evenly coated.
3. Evenly dividing them between the two zone, place the chicken drumsticks on the crisper plates.
4. In Zone 1, Select the AIR FRY function, set the temperature to 190°C, and set the time to 25-30 minutes. Select MATCH to duplicate settings across both zones. Press the START/STOP button to begin cooking.
5. Press the SYNC button to automatically sync the cook times of both zones.
6. After 15 minutes of cooking, open the drawers and flip the drumsticks to ensure even cooking.
7. Close the drawers and continue cooking until the chicken drumsticks are golden brown and cooked through with an internal temperature of 75°C.
8. Once cooked, remove the chicken drumsticks from the air fryer and let them rest for a few minutes before serving.
9. Serve the **Easy Cajun Chicken Drumsticks** with your favorite side dishes such as roasted vegetables, coleslaw, or a fresh salad.

CHICKEN PESTO PIZZAS | SERVES 4

Prep time: 15 min | Cook time: 12 min

- 4 small pizza bases or pita bread
- 4 tablespoons pesto sauce (60ml)
- 2 cooked chicken breasts, shredded
- 100g shredded mozzarella cheese
- 1/2 red onion, thinly sliced
- 1/2 red bell pepper, thinly sliced
- Handful of cherry tomatoes, halved
- Fresh basil leaves, for garnish
- Salt and pepper, to taste

DIRECTIONS:

1. Place the pizza bases or pita bread on a clean surface.
2. Spread 1 tablespoon of pesto sauce on each pizza base.
3. Divide the shredded chicken evenly among the pizza bases.
4. Sprinkle the shredded mozzarella cheese over the chicken.
5. Arrange the sliced red onion, red bell pepper, and cherry tomatoes on top of the cheese.
6. Season with salt and pepper to taste.
7. In each zone, place two pizzas on the crisper plate. Select the Zone 1, Select AIR FRY function, set the temperature to 200°C, and set the time to 10-12 minutes. Press the MATCH. Press the START/STOP button to begin cooking.
8. After 5 minutes of cooking, open the drawers and rotate the pizzas for even browning.
9. Close the drawers and continue cooking until the pizzas are golden brown and the cheese is melted and bubbly.
10. Once cooked, remove the pizzas from the air fryer and garnish with fresh basil leaves.
11. Serve the **Chicken Pesto Pizzas** hot and enjoy them as a delicious meal. You can customize the toppings according to your preferences, adding ingredients like mushrooms, olives, or fresh herbs.

TERIYAKI CHICKEN LEGS | SERVES 2

Prep time: 20 min | Cook time: 30 min

- 4 chicken legs
- 4 tablespoons soy sauce
- 2 tablespoons honey
- 1 tablespoon rice vinegar
- 1 tablespoon minced garlic
- 1 tablespoon grated ginger
- 1 tablespoon sesame oil
- 1 tablespoon cornstarch
- 2 tablespoons water
- Sesame seeds, for garnish
- Chopped spring onions, for garnish

DIRECTIONS:

1. In a bowl, mix together the soy sauce, honey, rice vinegar, minced garlic, grated ginger, and sesame oil to make the teriyaki sauce.
2. Place the chicken legs in a shallow dish and pour the teriyaki sauce over them, ensuring they are well coated. Let them marinate for about 10 minutes.
3. In Zone 1, place the chicken legs on the crisper plate. Select the AIR FRY function, set the temperature to 180°C, and set the time to 25-30 minutes. Press the START/STOP button to begin cooking.
4. After 15 minutes of cooking, open the drawers and flip the chicken legs to ensure even cooking.
5. In a small bowl, mix the cornstarch and water to create a slurry. Brush the slurry over the chicken legs to create a glaze.
6. Close the drawers and continue cooking until the chicken legs are cooked through and the skin is crispy.
7. Once cooked, remove the chicken legs from the air fryer and sprinkle with sesame seeds and chopped spring onions for garnish.
8. Serve the **Teriyaki Chicken Legs** hot with steamed rice or noodles and your choice of vegetables for a complete meal.

FRENCH GARLIC CHICKEN | SERVES 4

Prep time: 15 min | Cook time: 30 min

- 4 bone-in, skin-on chicken thighs
- 4 garlic cloves, minced
- 2 tablespoons butter, melted
- 2 tablespoons olive oil
- 2 tablespoons fresh lemon juice
- 1 teaspoon dried thyme
- 1 teaspoon dried rosemary
- Salt and pepper, to taste
- Fresh parsley, chopped for garnish

DIRECTIONS:

1. In a small bowl, mix together the minced garlic, melted butter, olive oil, lemon juice, dried thyme, dried rosemary, salt, and pepper to make a marinade.
2. Place the chicken thighs in a shallow dish and pour the marinade over them, ensuring they are well coated. Let them marinate for about 10 minutes.
3. In Zone 1, place the chicken thighs on the crisper plate. Select the AIR FRY function, set the temperature to 180°C, and set the time to 25-30 minutes. Press the START/STOP button to begin cooking.
4. After 15 minutes of cooking, open the drawers and flip the chicken thighs to ensure even cooking. Continue cooking until the chicken thighs are cooked through and the skin is crispy.
5. Once cooked, remove the chicken thighs from the air fryer and garnish with fresh chopped parsley.
6. Serve the **French Garlic Chicken** hot with your choice of side dishes such as roasted potatoes, steamed vegetables, or a fresh salad.

CHICKEN CROQUETTES WITH CREOLE SAUCE | SERVES 4

Prep time: 20 min | Cook time: 20 min

INGREDIENTS

For the Chicken Croquettes:

- 500g cooked chicken breast, finely shredded
- 1 small onion, finely chopped
- 2 cloves of garlic, minced
- 2 tablespoons fresh parsley, chopped
- 1 teaspoon dried thyme
- 1 teaspoon paprika
- 1/2 teaspoon salt
- 1/4 teaspoon black pepper
- 2 eggs, beaten
- 50g breadcrumbs
- 50g all-purpose flour
- Cooking spray

For the Creole Sauce:

- 2 tablespoons butter
- 1 small onion, finely chopped
- 1 small green bell pepper, finely chopped
- 2 cloves of garlic, minced
- 1 can (400g) diced tomatoes
- 1 teaspoon paprika
- 1/2 teaspoon dried oregano
- 1/4 teaspoon cayenne pepper (adjust according to your spice preference)
- Salt and pepper, to taste.

DIRECTIONS

1. In a mixing bowl, combine the shredded chicken, chopped onion, minced garlic, fresh parsley, dried thyme, paprika, salt, and black pepper. Mix well.
2. Shape the chicken mixture into small croquettes.
3. Place the beaten eggs, flour, and breadcrumbs in separate bowls for coating.
4. Dip each chicken croquette in the flour, then the beaten eggs, and finally coat with breadcrumbs.
5. Evenly dividing them (to cook in both zone) and place the chicken croquettes on the crisper plates.
6. In Zone 1, Select the AIR FRY function, set the temperature to 180°C, and set the time to 20 minutes. Press the MATCH. Press the START/STOP button to begin cooking.
7. In the meantime, prepare the Creole sauce. In a saucepan, melt the butter over medium heat. Add the chopped onion, green bell pepper, and minced garlic. Sauté until softened.
8. Add the diced tomatoes, paprika, dried oregano, cayenne pepper, salt, and pepper to the saucepan. Stir well and let it simmer for about 10 minutes, until the flavors meld together.
9. After 10 minutes of cooking the chicken croquettes, open the drawers and flip them to ensure even cooking. Spray them with cooking spray for a crispier texture.
10. Close the drawers and continue cooking until the chicken croquettes are golden brown and cooked through.
11. Once cooked, remove the chicken croquettes from the air fryer and serve them hot with the prepared Creole sauce on the side.
12. Enjoy the **Chicken Croquettes with Creole Sauce** as a delicious appetizer or main course.

CHICKEN AND BROCCOLI CASSEROLE | SERVES 4

Prep time: 15 min | Cook time: 20 min

INGREDIENTS

- 2 boneless, skinless chicken breasts, cooked and shredded
- 200g broccoli florets, steamed
- 100g grated cheddar cheese
- 120ml sour cream
- 120ml mayonnaise
- 25g grated Parmesan cheese

- 2 cloves garlic, minced
- 1/2 teaspoon dried thyme
- 1/2 teaspoon dried oregano
- 1/2 teaspoon salt
- 1/4 teaspoon black pepper

DIRECTIONS

1. In a large mixing bowl, combine the shredded chicken, steamed broccoli florets, grated cheddar cheese, sour cream, mayonnaise, grated Parmesan cheese, minced garlic, dried thyme, dried oregano, salt, and black pepper. Mix well until all the ingredients are evenly combined.
2. Transfer the chicken and broccoli mixture into a greased baking dish that fits into the Zone 1.
3. Place the baking dish into Zone 1 of the air fryer. Select the AIR FRY function, set the temperature to 180°C, and set the cooking time to 20 minutes.
4. Once cooking time is complete, check if the casserole is fully heated through and the cheese is melted and bubbly? Cook for an additional 5 minutes, if need.
5. Carefully remove the **Chicken and Broccoli Casserole** from the air fryer and let it cool for a few minutes before serving.

CHEESE-ENCRUSTED CHICKEN TENDERLOINS WITH PEANUTS | SERVES 4

Prep time: 15 min | Cook time: 15 min

- 500g chicken tenderloins
- 100g grated Parmesan cheese
- 100g breadcrumbs
- 50g roasted peanuts, crushed
- 2 eggs, beaten
- 2 tablespoons olive oil
- 1 teaspoon dried thyme
- 1/2 teaspoon garlic powder
- Salt and pepper, to taste

DIRECTIONS:

1. In a shallow bowl, combine the grated Parmesan cheese, breadcrumbs, crushed peanuts, dried thyme, garlic powder, salt, and pepper. Mix well.
2. Dip each chicken tenderloin into the beaten eggs, allowing any excess to drip off.
3. Coat the egg-coated chicken tenderloin with the cheese, breadcrumb, and peanut mixture, pressing gently to adhere the coating to the chicken.
4. Repeat the process with the remaining chicken tenderloins.
5. In Zone 1, place the coated chicken tenderloins on the crisper plate. Select the AIR FRY function, set the temperature to 200°C, and set time to 15 minutes. Press the START/STOP button to begin cooking.
6. While the chicken tenderloins are cooking, prepare any desired sauce or dip to accompany the dish.
7. After the cooking time is complete, remove the chicken tenderloins from the air fryer and let them cool for a few minutes before serving.
8. Enjoy the **Cheese-Encrusted Chicken Tenderloins with Peanuts** as a flavorful and crispy dish.

BACON-WRAPPED CHICKEN BREASTS ROLLS | SERVES 4

Prep time: 15 min | Cook time: 20 min

- 4 boneless, skinless chicken breasts
- 8 slices of streaky bacon
- 100g cream cheese
- 1 teaspoon garlic powder
- 1 teaspoon dried thyme
- Salt and pepper, to taste
- Toothpicks (for securing)

DIRECTIONS:

1. Pound the chicken breasts to flatten them slightly, making them easier to roll.
2. In a small bowl, mix the cream cheese, garlic powder, dried thyme, salt, and pepper.
3. Spread a spoonful of the cream cheese mixture onto each chicken breast.
4. Roll up each chicken breast tightly, starting from one end.
5. Wrap two slices of streaky bacon around each rolled chicken breast, securing them with toothpicks.
6. In Zone 1, place the bacon-wrapped chicken breast rolls on the crisper plate. Select the AIR FRY function, set the temperature to 200°C, and set the time to 18-20 minutes. Press the START/STOP.
7. After the cooking time is complete, remove the bacon-wrapped chicken breast rolls from the air fryer and let them cool for a few minutes.
8. Carefully remove the toothpicks before serving.
9. Enjoy the **Bacon-Wrapped Chicken Breast Rolls** as a delicious and satisfying dish. Serve them with your favorite sides, such as roasted vegetables or a fresh salad, for a complete meal.

GINGER TURMERIC CHICKEN THIGHS | SERVES 4

Prep time: 30 min | Cook time: 25 min

- 8 chicken thighs, bone-in, skin-on
- 2 tablespoons olive oil
- 2 tablespoons soy sauce
- 2 tablespoons honey
- 1 tablespoon grated ginger
- 1 teaspoon ground turmeric
- 1 teaspoon garlic powder
- Salt and pepper, to taste
- Fresh cilantro or parsley, for garnish (optional)

DIRECTIONS:

1. In a bowl, whisk together the olive oil, soy sauce, honey, grated ginger, ground turmeric, garlic powder, salt, and pepper to make the marinade.
2. Place the chicken thighs in a large resealable plastic bag or a bowl. Pour the marinade over the chicken and ensure they are well coated. Let the chicken marinate for at least 15 minutes or up to overnight in the refrigerator for more flavor.
3. Evenly dividing them to cook in two zone. Place the chicken thighs on two crisper plates, skin side down
4. Select Zone 1, Select the AIR FRY function, set the temperature to 180°C, and set the time to 10 minutes. Press MATCH. Press the START/STOP button to begin cooking.
5. After 10 minutes, flip the chicken thighs skin side up. Select the AIR FRY function, set the temperature to 180°C, and set the time to an additional 10-15 minutes, Press the START/STOP button to continue cooking.
6. Once the **chicken thighs** are cooked, remove them from the air fryer and let them rest for a few minutes.
7. Garnish with fresh cilantro or parsley, if desired, before serving.

LEMON THYME ROASTED CHICKEN | SERVES 5

Prep time: 15 min | Cook time: 60 min

- 1 whole chicken (approximately 1.6 kg), giblets removed (or choose a chicken with a weight suitable for 1 zone of your air fryer)
- 2 lemons, divided
- A handful of fresh thyme sprigs
- 4 cloves of garlic, minced
- 2 tablespoons olive oil
- Salt and pepper, to taste

DIRECTIONS:

1. Rinse the chicken inside and out with cold water and pat dry with paper towels.
2. Cut one lemon into slices and stuff them, along with a handful of fresh thyme sprigs, into the cavity of the chicken.
3. In a small bowl, combine the minced garlic, juice of the remaining lemon, olive oil, salt, and pepper to make a marinade.
4. Rub the marinade all over the chicken, ensuring it is evenly coated.
5. In Zone 1, place the chicken on the crisper plate, breast side up. Select the AIR FRY function, set the temperature to 180°C, and set the time to 30 minutes.
6. Press the START/STOP button to begin cooking.
7. After 30 minutes, carefully flip the chicken breast side down. Select the AIR FRY function, set the temperature to 180°C, and set the time to an additional 30 minutes.
8. Press the START/STOP button to resume cooking.
9. Once the cooking time is complete, check the internal temperature of the chicken using a meat thermometer. It should register at least 75°C to ensure it is fully cooked.
10. If needed, cook for additional time until the chicken reaches the desired temperature.
11. Once cooked, remove the chicken from the air fryer and let it rest for a few minutes before carving.
12. Serve the **Lemon Thyme Roasted Chicken** with your choice of side dishes, such as roasted potatoes, steamed vegetables, or a fresh salad.
13. The chicken will be juicy, tender, and infused with the delightful flavors of lemon and thyme.

Chapter 6: Beef, Pork, and Lamb

GREEK PORK WITH TZATZIKI SAUCE | SERVES 4

Prep time: 15 min | Cook time: 15 min

For the Greek Pork:

- 500g pork tenderloin, sliced into thin strips
- 2 tablespoons olive oil
- 2 cloves garlic, minced
- 1 teaspoon dried oregano
- 1 teaspoon dried thyme
- 1 teaspoon paprika
- Salt and pepper, to taste

For the Tzatziki Sauce:

- 200g Greek yogurt
- 1 cucumber, grated and squeezed to remove excess liquid
- 2 cloves garlic, minced
- 1 tablespoon fresh lemon juice
- 1 tablespoon chopped fresh dill
- Salt and pepper, to taste

For serving:

- Pita bread or rice
- Sliced tomatoes
- Sliced red onions
- Fresh parsley, for garnish

DIRECTIONS

1. In a bowl, combine the sliced pork, olive oil, minced garlic, dried oregano, dried thyme, paprika, salt, and pepper. Toss to coat the pork evenly with the seasonings.
2. Place the marinated pork slices in Zone 1 of the air fryer.
3. Select Zone 1, Select the AIR FRY function, set the temperature to 180°C, and set the cooking time to 13-15 minutes. Start the cooking process.
4. While the pork is cooking, prepare the Tzatziki sauce. In a separate bowl, combine the Greek yogurt, grated cucumber, minced garlic, lemon juice, chopped dill, salt, and pepper. Mix well to combine.
5. Once the pork is cooked and slightly browned, transfer it to a serving plate.
6. Serve the **Greek pork** with pita bread or rice, sliced tomatoes, sliced red onions, and a generous dollop of **Tzatziki sauce**. Garnish with fresh parsley.

Note: You can add additional toppings such as feta cheese, olives, or cucumber slices to customize your Greek pork dish.

ROAST BEEF WITH HORSERADISH CREAM | SERVES 6

Prep time: 15 min | Cook time: 40 min

- 1.2 kg beef roast
  (such as topside, sirloin, or rib-eye)
- 2 tablespoons olive oil
- 1 tablespoon Dijon mustard
- 2 cloves garlic, minced
- 1 tablespoon fresh rosemary, chopped
- Salt and pepper, to taste

For the Horseradish Cream:

- 200g sour cream
- 2 tablespoons prepared horseradish
- 1 tablespoon fresh lemon juice
- Salt and pepper, to taste

For serving:

- Roasted vegetables (such as potatoes, carrots, and parsnips)
- Fresh parsley, for garnish

DIRECTIONS

1. In a small bowl, combine the olive oil, Dijon mustard, minced garlic, chopped rosemary, salt, and pepper.
2. Place the beef roast in both zone of the air fryer.
3. Spread the olive oil and mustard mixture evenly over the beef, coating it on all sides.
4. Select Zone 1, Select the ROAST, function, set the temperature to 200°C, and set the cooking time to 30-40 minutes, depending on your preferred level of doneness (30 minutes for medium-rare, 35 minutes for medium, or 40 minutes for medium-well). Select MATCH to duplicate settings across both zones. Press the START/STOP button to begin cooking.
5. While the beef is cooking, prepare the horseradish cream. In a bowl, combine the sour cream, horseradish, lemon juice, salt, and pepper. Mix well to combine.
6. Once the beef is cooked to your desired level, remove it from the air fryer and let it rest for a few minutes before slicing.
7. Slice the **roast beef** and serve it with roasted vegetables and a dollop of **horseradish cream**. Garnish with fresh parsley.

Note: Cooking times may vary depending on the size and thickness of your beef roast. It's recommended to use a meat thermometer to ensure the desired level of doneness.

CHORIZO AND BEEF BURGER | SERVES 4

Prep time: 15 min | Cook time: 15 min

- 300g beef mince
- 100g chorizo, finely chopped
- 1 small onion, finely chopped
- 2 cloves of garlic, minced
- 1 teaspoon smoked paprika
- 1 teaspoon dried oregano
- Salt and pepper, to taste
- 4 burger buns
- Lettuce leaves
- Tomato slices
- Red onion slices
- Cheese slices (optional)
- Condiments of your choice (such as ketchup, mayonnaise, or mustard)

DIRECTIONS:

1. In a bowl, combine the beef mince, chopped chorizo, onion, garlic, smoked paprika, dried oregano, salt, and pepper. Mix well to combine all the ingredients.
2. Divide the mixture into four equal portions and shape them into burger patties.
3. Place the burger patties in Zone 1 of the air fryer. Select Zone 1, then select the AIR FRY function. Set the temperature to 200°C and the time to 15 minutes. Press the START/STOP button to begin cooking. Flipping halfway through, until the burgers are cooked through and nicely browned.
4. While the burgers are cooking, you can lightly toast the burger buns if desired.
5. Assemble the burgers by placing lettuce leaves, tomato slices, and red onion slices on the bottom half of each burger bun. If using cheese, place a cheese slice on top of the burger patty.
6. Once the burgers are cooked, place them on the prepared burger buns. Add your desired condiments on top.
7. Serve the **Chorizo and Beef Burgers** immediately with your favorite side dishes.

ITALIAN SAUSAGE AND CHEESE MEATBALLS I SERVES 4

Prep time: 15 min | Cook time: 15 min

- 500g Italian sausage meat
- 50g breadcrumbs
- 25g grated Parmesan cheese
- 25g finely chopped parsley
- 1/2 teaspoon garlic powder
- 1/2 teaspoon dried oregano
- 1/4 teaspoon salt
- 1/4 teaspoon black pepper
- 25g grated mozzarella cheese
- Marinara sauce, for serving

DIRECTIONS:

1. In a large mixing bowl, combine the Italian sausage meat, breadcrumbs, grated Parmesan cheese, chopped parsley, garlic powder, dried oregano, salt, and black pepper. Mix well until all ingredients are evenly incorporated.
2. Take a small portion of the meat mixture and flatten it in the palm of your hand. Place a small amount (about 1/4 teaspoon) of grated mozzarella cheese in the center. Fold the meat mixture around the cheese, shaping it into a ball. Repeat this process with the remaining meat mixture and cheese.
3. Once the air fryer has preheated, place the meatballs in Zone 1 of the air fryer. Select Zone 1, then select the AIR FRY function. Set the temperature to 180°C and the time to 15 minutes. Press the START/STOP button to begin cooking.
4. Cook the meatballs until they are golden brown and cooked through, with an internal temperature of 75°C. You can check the doneness by cutting one meatball open to ensure it's fully cooked.
5. Once cooked, remove the meatballs from the air fryer and let them cool slightly. Serve the **meatballs with marinara sauce** for dipping or as a topping.

MARINATED STEAK TIPS WITH MUSHROOMS | SERVES 4

Prep time: 70 min | Cook time: 12 min

- 500g steak tips, cut into bite-sized pieces
- 200g mushrooms, sliced
- 3 tablespoons olive oil
- 2 tablespoons Worcestershire sauce
- 2 tablespoons soy sauce
- 2 tablespoons balsamic vinegar
- 2 cloves garlic, minced
- 1 teaspoon Dijon mustard
- 1 teaspoon dried thyme
- Salt and pepper, to taste
- Fresh parsley, chopped (for garnish)

DIRECTIONS:

1. In a bowl, combine the olive oil, Worcestershire sauce, soy sauce, balsamic vinegar, minced garlic, Dijon mustard, dried thyme, salt, and pepper. Mix well to make the marinade.
2. Place the steak tips in a shallow dish and pour the marinade over them. Make sure the steak tips are well coated. Cover the dish and marinate in the refrigerator for at least 1 hour, or overnight for best flavor.
3. In Zone 1, place the marinated steak tips along with the mushrooms. Reserve any remaining marinade for later use.
4. Select Zone 1, select the ROAST function, and at 200°C, set the cooking time to 12 minutes. Press the START/STOP button to begin cooking.
5. While the steak tips are cooking, you can heat the reserved marinade in a small saucepan over medium heat until it comes to a simmer. Let it simmer for a few minutes to thicken slightly.
6. Once the cooking time is complete, carefully remove the steak tips and mushrooms from the air fryer.
7. Serve the marinated steak tips and mushrooms on a plate, drizzle with the heated marinade, and garnish with freshly chopped parsley.
8. Enjoy the flavorful **Marinated Steak Tips with Mushrooms** with your favorite side dishes or a fresh salad.

CHEESE PORK CHOPS | SERVES 4

Prep time: 10 min | Cook time: 15 min

- 4 pork chops
- 100g grated cheddar cheese
- 2 tablespoons breadcrumbs
- 1 tablespoon olive oil
- 1 teaspoon dried thyme
- 1/2 teaspoon garlic powder
- Salt and pepper, to taste

DIRECTIONS:

1. Preheat the Ninja Dual Zone Air Fryer by selecting Zone 1, then selecting the AIR FRY function. Set the temperature to 180°C and the time to 3 minutes. Press the START/STOP button to begin preheating.
2. In a shallow dish, combine the grated cheddar cheese, breadcrumbs, dried thyme, garlic powder, salt, and pepper.
3. Brush the pork chops with olive oil on both sides.
4. Dip each pork chop into the cheese and breadcrumb mixture, pressing firmly to coat both sides evenly.
5. Once the air fryer has preheated, place the pork chops in Zone 1. Select Zone 1, then select the AIR FRY function. Set the temperature to 180°C and the time to 12-15 minutes. Press the START/STOP button to begin cooking.
6. Flip the pork chops halfway through the cooking time to ensure even browning and cooking.
7. Cook the pork chops until they reach an internal temperature of 63°C and the cheese is melted and golden brown.
8. Once cooked, remove the pork chops from the air fryer and let them rest for a few minutes before serving.
9. Serve the **cheese pork chops** with your choice of sides, such as roasted vegetables, mashed potatoes, or a fresh salad.

CHICKEN FRIED STEAK WITH CREAM GRAVY | SERVES 4

Prep time: 15 min | Cook time: 15 min

For the Chicken Fried Steak:

- 4 beef cube steaks
- 100g all-purpose flour
- 1 teaspoon paprika
- 1/2 teaspoon garlic powder
- 1/2 teaspoon onion powder
- 1/2 teaspoon dried thyme
- Salt and pepper, to taste
- 2 eggs, beaten
- Vegetable oil, for frying

For the Cream Gravy:

- 2 tablespoons butter
- 2 tablespoons all-purpose flour
- 250ml whole milk
- Salt and pepper, to taste

DIRECTIONS

1. In a shallow dish, combine the all-purpose flour, paprika, garlic powder, onion powder, dried thyme, salt, and pepper.
2. Dip each beef cube steak into the beaten eggs, then coat it in the flour mixture, pressing firmly to adhere the coating to the steak. Repeat the process for all the steaks.
3. Once the air fryer has preheated, place the coated steaks in Zone 1. Select Zone 1, then select the AIR FRY function. Set the temperature to 200°C and the time to 15 minutes. Press the START/STOP button to begin cooking (if coated steaks don't fit in zone 1, use cook on both zones, don't forget to use the MATCH button).
4. While the steaks are cooking, prepare the cream gravy. In a saucepan, melt the butter over medium heat. Add the all-purpose flour and cook for 1-2 minutes, stirring constantly, until the mixture turns golden brown.
5. Gradually whisk in the whole milk, ensuring there are no lumps. Cook the mixture, stirring constantly, until the gravy thickens. Season with salt and pepper to taste. Remove from heat and set aside.
6. Flip the steaks halfway through the cooking time to ensure even browning and cooking.
7. Once the steaks are cooked and golden brown, remove them from the air fryer and let them rest for a few minutes.
8. Serve the chicken fried steaks with the cream gravy poured over the top. They are traditionally enjoyed with mashed potatoes and steamed vegetables.
9. Enjoy the comforting and delicious **chicken fried steak with creamy gravy** !

REUBEN BEEF ROLLS WITH THOUSAND ISLAND SAUCE | MAKES 10 ROLLS

Prep time: 20 min | Cook time: 20 min

- 500g thinly sliced roast beef
- 200g sauerkraut
- 10 slices Swiss cheese
- 10 slices rye bread
- 120ml Thousand Island dressing
- Butter, for brushing

DIRECTIONS:

1. Lay out the rye bread slices and brush one side of each slice with butter.
2. On each bread slice, layer a slice of Swiss cheese, a portion of roast beef, a spoonful of sauerkraut, and a drizzle of Thousand Island dressing.
3. Roll up the bread slices tightly and secure with toothpicks.
4. Place the beef rolls in both zone of the air fryer basket.
5. Select Zone 1, choose the AIR FRY function, set the temperature to 200°C, and the time to 15 minutes. Select MATCH. Press the START/STOP.
6. While the beef rolls are cooking, prepare the dipping sauce by combining the remaining Thousand Island dressing with any desired additional seasonings.
7. After 15 minutes, carefully remove the beef rolls from the air fryer and let them cool slightly.
8. Serve the **Reuben beef rolls with the Thousand Island dipping sauce**.

For Thousand Island Sauce:

- 120 ml mayonnaise
- 30 ml ketchup
- 15 ml sweet pickle relish
- 15 ml finely chopped onion
- 5 ml white vinegar
- 5 ml Worcestershire sauce
- Salt and pepper to taste.

Directions:

- In a bowl, combine the mayonnaise, ketchup, sweet pickle relish, chopped onion, white vinegar, and Worcestershire sauce.
- Mix well until all the ingredients are thoroughly combined. Season with salt and pepper to taste.
- Once prepared, refrigerate the Thousand Island sauce for at least 30 minutes to allow the flavors to meld together.

BEEF AND SPINACH ROLLS | SERVES 2

Prep time: 15 min | Cook time: 15 min

- 4 thin beef slices (such as sirloin or minute steaks)
- 60 g fresh spinach leaves
- 1/2 onion, thinly sliced
- 2 cloves garlic, minced
- 1 tablespoon olive oil
- Salt and pepper, to taste
- 1/2 teaspoon dried thyme
- Toothpicks

DIRECTIONS:

1. In a skillet, heat olive oil over medium heat. Add the minced garlic and sliced onion. Sauté until the onion becomes translucent and the garlic is fragrant.
2. Add the fresh spinach leaves to the skillet and cook until wilted. Season with salt, pepper, and dried thyme. Remove from heat and let the mixture cool slightly.
3. Lay out the beef slices on a clean surface. Divide the spinach and onion mixture equally among the beef slices, spreading it evenly.
4. Roll up each beef slice tightly and secure with toothpicks to hold the rolls together.
5. Place the beef rolls in Zone 1. Select Zone 1, then select the AIR FRY function. Set the temperature to 200°C and the time to 12-15 minutes. Press the START/STOP button to begin cooking.
6. Flip the beef rolls halfway through the cooking time to ensure even browning.
7. Once the beef rolls are cooked and golden brown, remove them from the air fryer and let them cool slightly.
8. Serve the **beef and spinach rolls** as a delicious appetizer or main dish. Remove the toothpicks before serving.

SUMPTUOUS PIZZA TORTILLA ROLLS | SERVES 4

Prep time: 15 min | Cook time: 10 min

- 4 large flour tortillas
- 125 ml tomato sauce
- 100 g shredded mozzarella cheese
- 30 g sliced pepperoni
- 30 g sliced black olives
- 30 g sliced red bell pepper
- 30 g sliced mushrooms
- 1/4 teaspoon dried oregano
- 1/4 teaspoon garlic powder
- Salt and pepper, to taste.

DIRECTIONS:

1. Lay out one tortilla on a clean surface. Spread a thin layer of tomato sauce evenly over the tortilla, leaving a small border around the edges.
2. Sprinkle 25 g of shredded mozzarella cheese over the tomato sauce.
3. Add 7.5 g of pepperoni slices, black olives, red bell pepper, and mushrooms on top of the cheese.
4. Sprinkle a pinch of dried oregano, garlic powder, salt, and pepper over the toppings.
5. Roll up the tortilla tightly, starting from one end. Repeat the process for the remaining tortillas and fillings.
6. Place the tortilla rolls in both zone. Select Zone 1, then select the AIR FRY function. Set the temperature to 180°C and the time to 10 minutes. Select MACTH. Press the START/STOP button to begin cooking.
7. Flip the tortilla rolls halfway through the cooking time to ensure even browning.
8. Once the tortilla rolls are golden brown and crispy, remove them from the air fryer and let them cool slightly.
9. Cut each tortilla roll into bite-sized pieces and serve as a delicious appetizer or snack.
10. Enjoy the **sumptuous pizza tortilla rolls**!

Note: Feel free to customize the toppings according to your preferences. Adjust the cooking time if needed to achieve your desired level of crispness.

BACON-WRAPPED CHEESE PORK | SERVES 4

Prep time: 15 min | Cook time: 20 min

- 4 boneless pork chops (about 150g each)
- 8 slices of bacon
- 100g cheddar cheese, cut into thin strips
- 1 teaspoon dried thyme
- 1/2 teaspoon garlic powder
- Salt and pepper, to taste
- Cooking oil spray

DIRECTIONS:

1. Preheat Zone 1 of the Ninja Dual Zone air fryer to 200°C for 5 minutes.
2. Meanwhile, season the pork chops with dried thyme, garlic powder, salt, and pepper. Wrap each pork chop with 2 slices of bacon, securing them with toothpicks if needed.
3. Place the bacon-wrapped pork chops in Zone 1 of the air fryer. Select Zone 1, choose the AIR FRY program, set the temperature to 200°C, and set the time to 15 minutes. Press the START/STOP button to begin cooking.
4. In the meantime, prepare the cheese filling. Take each pork chop and make a small incision in the side. Insert the thin strips of cheddar cheese into the incision, distributing evenly among the pork chops.
5. After 15 minutes of cooking, open the air fryer and carefully flip the bacon-wrapped pork chops using tongs. Return them to Zone 1 and continue cooking for an additional 5 minutes.
6. Once the cooking time is complete, remove the bacon-wrapped cheese pork from the air fryer. Allow them to rest for a few minutes before serving.
7. Serve the **Bacon-Wrapped Cheese Pork** hot with your choice of sides, such as mashed potatoes or a green salad.

BEAN AND BEEF MEATBALL TACO PIZZA | SERVES 4

Prep time: 20 min | Cook time: 15 min

For the Meatballs:

- 300g lean ground beef
- 60g breadcrumbs
- 25g grated Parmesan cheese
- 25g finely chopped onion
- 1 clove garlic, minced
- 1 teaspoon dried oregano
- 1/2 teaspoon ground cumin
- Salt and pepper, to taste

For the Taco Pizza:

- 4 small tortillas
- 120g refried beans
- 60g grated cheddar cheese
- 60g diced tomatoes
- 30g sliced black olives
- 15g chopped fresh cilantro
- Sour cream and salsa, for serving

DIRECTIONS

1. In a mixing bowl, combine the ground beef, breadcrumbs, Parmesan cheese, onion, garlic, dried oregano, ground cumin, salt, and pepper. Mix well until all ingredients are evenly incorporated.
2. Shape the meat mixture into small meatballs, about 2.5cm in diameter. Place the meatballs in Zone 1 of the air fryer. Select Zone 1, choose the AIR FRY program, set the temperature to 200°C, and set the time to 10 minutes. Press the START/STOP.
3. While the meatballs are cooking, prepare the taco pizza. Take each tortilla and spread a layer of refried beans on one side.
4. Place the tortillas with the refried beans in Zone 2.
5. Select Zone 2, choose the AIR FRY program, set the temperature to 180°C, and time to 5 minutes. Press the START/STOP.
6. After 5 minutes, open the air fryer and remove the tortillas with the refried beans from Zone 2. Sprinkle grated cheddar cheese, diced tomatoes, sliced black olives, and chopped cilantro on top of the tortillas.
7. Return the tortillas with the toppings to Zone 2 and continue cooking for an additional 5 minutes or until the cheese has melted and the tortillas are crispy.
8. Once the cooking time is complete, remove the taco pizzas and meatballs from the air fryer.
9. Serve the **Bean and Beef Meatball Taco Pizza** hot, topped with the cooked meatballs. Garnish with sour cream and salsa, if desired.

CAJUN BACON PORK LOIN FILLET | SERVES 6

Prep time: 15 min | Cook time: 25 min

- 1.2 kg pork loin fillet
- 8 slices bacon
- 2 tablespoons Cajun seasoning
- 2 tablespoons olive oil
- Salt and pepper, to taste.

DIRECTIONS:

1. Preheat both Zone of the Ninja Dual Zone air fryer to 200°C for 5 minutes.
2. Season the pork loin fillet with Cajun seasoning, salt, and pepper, ensuring it is evenly coated.
3. Wrap the seasoned pork loin fillet with bacon slices, securing them with toothpicks if necessary.
4. Drizzle olive oil over the bacon-wrapped pork loin fillet.
5. Place the pork loin fillet in both zone of the air fryer. Select Zone 1, choose the AIR FRY program, set the temperature to 200°C, and set the time to 25 minutes. Select MATCH to duplicate settings across both zones. Press the START/STOP button to begin cooking.
6. After 12 minutes of cooking, open the air fryer and carefully flip the pork loin fillet to ensure even browning.
7. Close the air fryer and continue cooking for the remaining time or until the internal temperature of the pork reaches 63°C. Adjust the cooking time as needed based on the thickness of the fillet.
8. Once cooked, remove the **Cajun Bacon Pork Loin Fillet** from the air fryer and let it rest for a few minutes before slicing.
9. Slice the pork loin fillet into thick slices and serve hot.

LEMON PORK WITH MARJORAM | SERVES 4

Prep time: 15 min | Cook time: 20 min

- 600g pork tenderloin, sliced into medallions
- Zest of 1 lemon
- Juice of 1 lemon
- 2 tablespoons olive oil
- 2 cloves garlic, minced
- 1 tablespoon fresh marjoram leaves, chopped
- Salt and pepper, to taste

DIRECTIONS:

1. In a bowl, combine the lemon zest, lemon juice, olive oil, minced garlic, chopped marjoram, salt, and pepper. Mix well to create a marinade.
2. Add the pork medallions to the marinade and toss to coat them evenly. Let them marinate for at least 10 minutes.
3. Place the marinated pork medallions in Zone 1 of the air fryer. Select Zone 1, choose the AIR FRY program, set the temperature to 200°C, and set the time to 20 minutes. Press the START/STOP button to begin cooking.
4. After 10 minutes of cooking, open the air fryer and carefully flip the pork medallions to ensure even cooking.
5. Close the air fryer and continue cooking for the remaining time or until the pork is cooked through and golden brown.
6. Once cooked, remove the Lemon Pork with Marjoram from the air fryer and let it rest for a few minutes before serving.
7. Serve the pork medallions with your choice of sides, such as roasted vegetables or a fresh salad.
8. Enjoy the zesty and flavorful **Lemon Pork with Marjoram** prepared in the Ninja Dual Zone air fryer. The combination of lemon, garlic, and marjoram adds a delicious twist to the pork medallions, making it a tasty and satisfying dish for any occasion.

BACON WRAPPED PORK WITH APPLE GRAVY | SERVES 4

Prep time: 15 min | Cook time: 25 min

- 4 pork tenderloin medallions (about 150g each)
- 8 slices of bacon
- 2 tablespoons olive oil
- 2 apples, peeled, cored, and diced
- 1 small onion, finely chopped
- 2 cloves of garlic, minced
- 250ml chicken or vegetable stock
- 2 tablespoons butter
- 2 tablespoons all-purpose flour
- Salt and pepper to taste

DIRECTIONS:

1. Wrap each pork tenderloin medallion with 2 slices of bacon, securing the bacon with toothpicks if needed.
2. Brush the bacon-wrapped pork with olive oil and season with salt and pepper.
3. Place the pork medallions in Zone 1 of the air fryer basket.
4. In Zone 2, add the diced apples, onion, and minced garlic. Toss to coat evenly.
5. Select Zone 1, choose the AIR FRY program, set the temperature to 200°C, and set the time to 25 minutes. Press the START/STOP button to begin cooking.
6. Select Zone 2, choose the ROAST program, set the temperature to 200°C, and set the time to 8-10 minutes. Press the START/STOP.
7. While the pork and apples are cooking, prepare the apple gravy. In a saucepan, melt the butter over medium heat. Add the flour and stir continuously for 1-2 minutes to make a roux.
8. Gradually whisk in the chicken or vegetable stock, cook for a few minutes until the mixture thickens.
9. Add the cooked apples, onion, and garlic from Zone 2 of the air fryer to the saucepan with the gravy. Stir well to combine. Season with salt and pepper to taste. Continue cooking the gravy over low heat for another 3-5 minutes, allowing the flavors to meld together.
10. Once the cooking time for the pork is complete, remove the **bacon-wrapped pork** medallions from Zone 1 of the air fryer and let them rest for a few minutes.
11. Drizzle the apple gravy over the pork chops and garnish with fresh chopped parsley. Enjoy!

ITALIAN SAUSAGE LINKS | SERVES 4

Prep time: 5 min | Cook time: 20 min

- 8 Italian sausage links
- 1 tablespoon olive oil
- 1 teaspoon dried oregano
- 1 teaspoon dried basil
- 1/2 teaspoon garlic powder
- 1/2 teaspoon onion powder
- Salt and pepper, to taste

DIRECTIONS:

1. In a small bowl, mix together the dried oregano, dried basil, garlic powder, onion powder, salt, and pepper.
2. Drizzle the olive oil over the Italian sausage links and rub them with the spice mixture to coat evenly.
3. Place the seasoned sausage links in Zone 1 of the air fryer. Select Zone 1, choose the AIR FRY program, set the temperature to 200°C, and set the time to 20 minutes. Press the START/STOP button to begin cooking.
4. After 10 minutes of cooking, carefully flip the sausage links using tongs to ensure even browning.
5. Once the cooking time is complete, remove the Italian sausage links from the air fryer.
6. Serve the **Italian sausage links** on a platter and enjoy them as they are, or use them in sandwiches, pasta dishes, or other recipes according to your preference.

These Italian Sausage Links prepared in the Ninja Dual Zone air fryer will be deliciously seasoned and have a crispy exterior. They can be enjoyed on their own or used in various dishes to add flavor and protein.

PORK MEDALLIONS WITH ENDIVE SALAD | SERVES 4

Prep time: 15 min | Cook time: 20 min

- 500g pork tenderloin, cut into medallions
- 2 tablespoons olive oil
- 2 cloves garlic, minced
- 1 teaspoon dried thyme
- Salt and pepper, to taste
- 2 endives, thinly sliced
- 1 small red onion, thinly sliced
- 100g cherry tomatoes, halved
- 50g feta cheese, crumbled
- 2 tablespoons lemon juice
- 2 tablespoons extra virgin olive oil.

DIRECTIONS:

1. In a bowl, combine the minced garlic, dried thyme, salt, pepper, and 1 tablespoon of olive oil. Mix well.
2. Place the pork medallions in a separate bowl and coat them with the garlic and thyme mixture.
3. Place the seasoned pork medallions in Zone 1 of the air fryer. Select Zone 1, choose the AIR FRY program, set the temperature to 200°C, and set the time to 10 minutes. Press the START/STOP button to begin cooking.
4. While the pork is cooking, prepare the endive salad. In a large bowl, combine the sliced endives, red onion, cherry tomatoes, and crumbled feta cheese.
5. In a small bowl, whisk together the lemon juice, extra virgin olive oil, salt, and pepper. Pour the dressing over the salad and toss to combine.
6. After 10 minutes of cooking, carefully flip the pork medallions using tongs and cook for another 5-8 minutes or until they reach an internal temperature of 63°C.
7. Remove the pork medallions from the air fryer and let them rest for a few minutes before serving.
8. Serve the **pork medallions alongside the refreshing endive salad**.

CHEESE CRUSTED PORK CHOPS | SERVES 4 TO 6

Prep time: 15 min | Cook time: 20 min

- 4 to 6 pork chops
- 120g breadcrumbs
- 120g grated cheddar cheese
- 1 teaspoon dried thyme
- 1 teaspoon paprika
- Salt and pepper, to taste
- 2 eggs, beaten
- Cooking spray

DIRECTIONS:

1. Preheat Zone 1 of the Ninja Dual Zone air fryer to 200°C for 5 minutes.
2. In a shallow bowl, combine the breadcrumbs, grated cheddar cheese, dried thyme, paprika, salt, and pepper. Mix well.
3. Dip each pork chop into the beaten eggs, making sure to coat both sides.
4. Press each pork chop into the breadcrumb and cheese mixture, ensuring a thick and even coating on both sides. Place the coated pork chops on a plate.
5. Spray Zone 1 of the air fryer with cooking spray to prevent sticking.
6. Place the cheese-crusted pork chops in Zone 1 of the air fryer. Select Zone 1, choose the AIR FRY program, set the temperature to 200°C, and set the time to 15 minutes. Press the START/STOP button to begin cooking.
7. After 15 minutes of cooking, carefully flip the pork chops using tongs and cook for another 5 minutes or until they reach an internal temperature of 71°C.
8. Remove the cheese-crusted pork chops from the air fryer and let them rest for a few minutes before serving.
9. Serve the **cheese-crusted pork chops** with your choice of sides, such as roasted vegetables or a fresh salad.

SOUTHERN CHILI | SERVES 4

Prep time: 15 min | Cook time: 30 min

- 500g ground beef
- 1 onion, diced
- 2 cloves of garlic, minced
- 1 red bell pepper, diced
- 1 can (400g) diced tomatoes
- 1 can (400g) kidney beans, drained and rinsed
- 1 tablespoon tomato paste
- 1 tablespoon chili powder
- 1 teaspoon ground cumin
- 1 teaspoon paprika
- 1/2 teaspoon dried oregano
- 1/2 teaspoon sugar
- Salt and pepper, to taste
- Optional toppings: grated cheese, sour cream, chopped green onions

DIRECTIONS:

1. In Zone 1 of the air fryer, add the ground beef, onion, garlic, and red bell pepper. Select Zone 1, choose the AIR FRY program, set the temperature to 200°C, and set the time to 10 minutes. Press the START/STOP button to begin cooking. Cook until the ground beef is browned and the vegetables are softened.
2. Drain any excess fat from the ground beef mixture.
3. In Zone 1 of the air fryer, keep adding the diced tomatoes, kidney beans, tomato paste, chili powder, ground cumin, paprika, dried oregano, sugar, salt, and pepper. Mix well.
4. Select Zone 1, choose the BAKE program, set the temperature to 180°C, and set the time to 20 minutes. Press the START/STOP button to begin cooking. Stir the chili mixture occasionally during cooking.
5. After 20 minutes of cooking, check the seasoning and adjust if needed.
6. Serve the **Southern Chili** hot, garnished with grated cheese, sour cream, and chopped green onions, if desired.

BACON AND CHEESE STUFFED PORK CHOPS | SERVES 4

Prep time: 15 min | Cook time: 25 min

- 4 boneless pork chops
- 4 slices of bacon
- 100g grated cheddar cheese
- 1 teaspoon dried thyme
- 1 teaspoon paprika
- Salt and pepper, to taste
- 1 tablespoon olive oil.

DIRECTIONS:

1. Preheat Zone 1 of the Ninja Dual Zone air fryer to 200°C for 5 minutes.
2. In a bowl, combine the grated cheddar cheese, dried thyme, paprika, salt, and pepper.
3. Using a sharp knife, make a deep pocket in each pork chop by cutting horizontally through the side.
4. Stuff each pork chop pocket with the cheese mixture.
5. Wrap each stuffed pork chop with a slice of bacon, securing it with toothpicks if necessary.
6. Brush the pork chops with olive oil on both sides.
7. Place the bacon-wrapped pork chops in Zone 1 of the air fryer. Select Zone 1, choose the AIR FRY program, set the temperature to 200°C, and set the time to 20-25 minutes. Press the START/STOP button to begin cooking. Cook until the pork chops are browned and cooked through, with an internal temperature of 70°C.
8. Once cooked, remove the pork chops from the air fryer and let them rest for a few minutes before serving.
9. Serve the **Bacon and Cheese Stuffed Pork Chops** hot, alongside your favorite side dishes like roasted vegetables, mashed potatoes, or a fresh salad.

MEAT AND RICE STUFFED PEPPERS | SERVES 4

Prep time: 15 min | Cook time: 25 min

- 4 large bell peppers (any color)
- 250g ground beef
- 1 small onion, finely chopped
- 1 garlic clove, minced
- 200g cooked rice
- 200g tomato passata
- 1 teaspoon dried oregano
- 1 teaspoon dried basil
- Salt and pepper, to taste
- 50g grated cheddar cheese.

DIRECTIONS:

1. Cut the tops off the bell peppers and remove the seeds and membranes. Set aside.
2. In a pan, cook the ground beef over medium heat until browned. Add the chopped onion and minced garlic, and cook until the onion is softened.
3. Add the cooked rice, tomato passata, dried oregano, dried basil, salt, and pepper to the pan. Stir well to combine all the ingredients and let the mixture simmer for a few minutes.
4. Spoon the meat and rice mixture into each bell pepper, filling them to the top.
5. Sprinkle grated cheddar cheese on top of each stuffed pepper.
6. Place the stuffed peppers in Zone 1 of the air fryer. Select Zone 1, choose the AIR FRY program, set the temperature to 180°C, and set the time to 20-25 minutes. Press the START/STOP button to begin cooking. Cook until the peppers are tender and the cheese is melted and golden.
7. Once cooked, remove the stuffed peppers from the air fryer and let them cool slightly before serving.
8. Serve the **Meat and Rice Stuffed Peppers** as a delicious main course. They can be enjoyed on their own or accompanied by a side salad or crusty bread.

SPICY RUMP STEAK | SERVES 4

Prep time: 10 min | Cook time: 15 min

- 4 rump steaks (approximately 200g each)
- 2 tablespoons olive oil
- 2 teaspoons paprika
- 1 teaspoon garlic powder
- 1 teaspoon onion powder
- 1 teaspoon cayenne pepper (adjust to taste)
- 1 teaspoon dried oregano
- 1 teaspoon dried thyme
- Salt and pepper, to taste
- Fresh parsley, for garnish (optional)

DIRECTIONS:

1. In a small bowl, mix together the paprika, garlic powder, onion powder, cayenne pepper, dried oregano, dried thyme, salt, and pepper to create a spice rub.
2. Rub the spice mixture onto both sides of each rump steak, ensuring they are evenly coated.
3. Drizzle the olive oil over the steaks and gently massage it into the meat.
4. Place the seasoned rump steaks in Zone 1 of the air fryer. (If too crowded, place and cook in both zone)
5. Select Zone 1, choose the ROAST program, set the temperature to 200°C, and set time to 10-15 minutes, depending on your desired level of doneness. Press the START/STOP button to begin cooking.
6. After 5-7 minutes, flip the steaks over using tongs to ensure even cooking.
7. Continue cooking for the remaining time or until the steaks reach your desired level of doneness. For medium-rare, aim for an internal temperature of 55-60°C. Adjust the cooking time accordingly if you prefer your steaks more or less cooked.
8. Once cooked, remove the steaks from the air fryer and let them rest for a few minutes before slicing.
9. Garnish with fresh parsley, if desired, and serve the **Spicy Rump Steaks** hot. They can be enjoyed on their own or served with a side of roasted vegetables, mashed potatoes, or a crisp salad.

BEEF MINCE TACO ROLLS | SERVES 4

Prep time: 15 min | Cook time: 15 min

- 500g beef mince
- 1 small onion, finely diced
- 2 cloves garlic, minced
- 2 teaspoons chili powder
- 1 teaspoon ground cumin
- 1 teaspoon paprika
- 1/2 teaspoon dried oregano
- Salt and pepper, to taste
- 4 large tortilla wraps
- 100g grated cheddar cheese
- Salsa, sour cream, and guacamole, for serving
- Fresh coriander (cilantro), for garnish (optional)

DIRECTIONS:

1. In a large skillet or frying pan, heat a little oil over medium heat. Add the diced onion and minced garlic, and cook until softened and translucent.
2. Add the beef mince to the pan and cook until browned, breaking it up with a spatula or spoon as it cooks.
3. Stir in the chili powder, ground cumin, paprika, dried oregano, salt, and pepper. Cook for another 2-3 minutes to allow the flavors to meld.
4. Remove the beef mince mixture from the heat and set aside.
5. Place one tortilla wrap on a clean surface. Spoon a portion of the beef mince mixture onto the center of the tortilla, spreading it out evenly.
6. Sprinkle grated cheddar cheese over the beef mince mixture.
7. Roll up the tortilla tightly, folding in the sides as you go. Repeat this process for the remaining tortillas and filling.
8. Place the taco rolls in Zone 1 of the air fryer. Select Zone 1, choose the AIR FRY program, set temperature to 180°C, and set time to 15 minutes. Press the START/STOP button to begin cooking.
9. After 6-8 minutes, flip the taco rolls over. Continue cooking for the remaining time or until the taco rolls are crispy and golden.
10. Once cooked, remove the taco rolls from the air fryer and let them cool for a few minutes.
11. Serve the **Beef Mince Taco Rolls** with salsa, sour cream, guacamole, and fresh coriander for garnish.

PORK KEBAB WITH YOGURT SAUCE | SERVES 4

Prep time: 20 min | Cook time: 15 min

For the Pork Kebabs:
- 500g pork tenderloin, cut into cubes
- 1 red onion, cut into chunks
- 1 red bell pepper, cut into chunks
- 1 green bell pepper, cut into chunks
- 2 tablespoons olive oil
- 2 tablespoons lemon juice
- 2 cloves garlic, minced
- 1 teaspoon ground cumin
- 1 teaspoon paprika
- 1/2 teaspoon dried oregano
- Salt and pepper, to taste
- Skewers (if using wooden skewers, soak them in water for 30 minutes before use)

For the Yogurt Sauce:
- 200g Greek yogurt
- 1 tablespoon lemon juice
- 1 tablespoon chopped fresh mint
- Salt and pepper, to taste

DIRECTIONS:

1. In a bowl, combine the olive oil, lemon juice, minced garlic, ground cumin, paprika, dried oregano, salt, and pepper. Mix well to create a marinade.
2. Add the pork tenderloin cubes to the marinade and toss to coat them evenly. Let the pork marinate for at least 10 minutes to absorb the flavors.
3. Thread the marinated pork cubes onto skewers, alternating with chunks of red onion and bell peppers.
4. Place the pork kebabs in Zone 1 of the air fryer. Select Zone 1, choose the AIR FRY program, set the temperature to 200°C, and set time to 15 minutes. Press the START/STOP button to begin cooking. (If too crowded, place and cook in both zone). After 8 minutes, flip the kebabs rolls over.
5. While the kebabs are cooking, prepare the yogurt sauce. In a small bowl, combine the Greek yogurt, lemon juice, chopped fresh mint, salt, and pepper. Stir well to combine.
6. Once the kebabs are cooked and nicely browned, remove them from the air fryer.
7. Serve the **Pork Kebabs hot with the yogurt sauce** on the side.

FISH CAKES
| SERVES 4

INGREDIENTS:

- 400g white fish fillets (such as cod or haddock)
- 500g potatoes, peeled and diced
- 1 small onion, finely chopped
- 2 tablespoons chopped fresh parsley
- 1 tablespoon lemon juice
- 1 teaspoon Dijon mustard
- Salt and pepper to taste
- 2 eggs, beaten
- 100g breadcrumbs
- Vegetable oil, for brushing.

Prep time: 20 min | Cook time: 15 min

DIRECTIONS

1. Place the fish fillets in Zone 1 of the air fryer. Select Zone 1, select the AIR FRY function, set the temperature to 200°C and set the cooking time to 10 minutes. Press the START/STOP button to begin cooking. Once cooked, remove the fish fillets from the air fryer and let them cool slightly.
2. Meanwhile, boil the diced potatoes in a pot of salted water until tender. Drain and mash the potatoes.
3. In a bowl, flake the cooked fish fillets into small pieces. Add the mashed potatoes, chopped onion, parsley, lemon juice, Dijon mustard, salt, and pepper. Mix well to combine.
4. Shape the mixture into fish cakes of your desired size.
5. Dip each fish cake into the beaten eggs, then coat with breadcrumbs.
6. Place the fish cakes in Zone 1 of the air fryer. Select Zone 1, select the AIR FRY function, set the temperature to 200°C, and set the cooking time to 12-15 minutes. Press the START/STOP button to begin cooking.
7. While the fish cakes are cooking, lightly brush them with vegetable oil halfway through the cooking process to promote browning and crispiness.
8. Once the cooking time is complete, remove the fish cakes from the air fryer and let them cool slightly before serving.
9. Serve the **fish cakes** hot with tartar sauce or a squeeze of lemon juice. They can be enjoyed with a side of salad or steamed vegetables.

CRISPY FISH STICKS | SERVES 4

Prep time: 15 min | Cook time: 12 min

- 500g white fish fillets (such as cod or haddock), cut into finger-sized strips
- 100g all-purpose flour
- 2 eggs, beaten
- 150g breadcrumbs
- 1 teaspoon paprika
- 1/2 teaspoon garlic powder
- Salt and pepper to taste
- Lemon wedges, for serving
- Tartar sauce or ketchup, for dipping

DIRECTIONS:

1. Preheat the Zone 1 to the AIR FRY program at 200°C.
2. Place the flour, beaten eggs, and breadcrumbs in separate shallow bowls. Season the flour with salt, pepper, paprika, and garlic powder, and mix well.
3. Dip each fish strip into the seasoned flour, shaking off any excess.
4. Dip the floured fish strip into the beaten eggs, allowing any excess to drip off.
5. Coat the fish strip with breadcrumbs, pressing gently to adhere.
6. Repeat the coating process for the remaining fish strips.
7. Place the coated fish sticks in Zone 1 of the air fryer. Select Zone 1, select the AIR FRY function, set temperature to 200°C and cooking time 12 minutes. Press the START/STOP.
8. Halfway through the cooking process, carefully flip the fish sticks to ensure even browning.
9. Once the cooking time is complete, remove the fish sticks from the air fryer and let them cool slightly before serving.
10. Serve the crispy fish sticks with lemon wedges and your choice of tartar sauce or ketchup for dipping.
11. Enjoy the delicious and **crispy fish sticks** as a snack, appetizer, or main dish.

SOLE AND CAULIFLOWER FRITTERS | SERVES 2

Prep time: 20 min | Cook time: 10 min

- 200g sole fillets, boneless and skinless
- 200g cauliflower florets
- 1 small onion, finely chopped
- 2 cloves garlic, minced
- 2 tablespoons fresh parsley, finely chopped
- 1 teaspoon lemon zest
- 2 eggs, beaten
- 50g breadcrumbs
- Salt and pepper to taste
- Vegetable oil spray.

DIRECTIONS:

1. Steam the cauliflower florets until tender. Drain and allow them to cool.
2. In a food processor, pulse the sole fillets, steamed cauliflower, chopped onion, minced garlic, fresh parsley, and lemon zest until well combined but still slightly chunky.
3. Transfer the mixture to a bowl and add the beaten eggs, breadcrumbs, salt, and pepper. Mix until everything is evenly incorporated.
4. Shape the mixture into small fritters, about the size of a golf ball.
5. Place the fritters in Zone 1 of the air fryer. Select Zone 1, select the AIR FRY function, set temperature to 200°C, set the cooking time to 10 minutes. Press the START/STOP.
6. Halfway through the cooking process, carefully flip the fritters to ensure even browning.
7. Once the cooking time is complete, remove the fritters from the air fryer and let them cool slightly before serving.
8. Lightly spray the fritters with vegetable oil spray to enhance their crispiness.
9. Serve the sole and cauliflower fritters as a delicious and nutritious appetizer or main dish.
10. You can accompany the fritters with a side of mixed greens or a dip of your choice, such as tartar sauce or lemon aioli.
11. This recipe for **sole and cauliflower fritters** is tailored to the taste preferences of the UK people, who enjoy flavorful and crispy fritters.

PRAWN DEJONGHE SKEWERS | SERVES 4

Prep time: 20 min | Cook time: 10 min

- 500g large prawns, peeled and deveined
- 4 cloves garlic, minced
- 2 tablespoons fresh parsley, finely chopped
- 2 tablespoons breadcrumbs
- 2 tablespoons grated Parmesan cheese
- 2 tablespoons melted butter
- 1 tablespoon lemon juice
- Salt and pepper to taste
- Vegetable oil spray
- Skewers (soaked in water if using wooden skewers)

DIRECTIONS:

1. In a bowl, combine the minced garlic, fresh parsley, breadcrumbs, grated Parmesan cheese, melted butter, lemon juice, salt, and pepper. Mix well to create a flavorful coating.
2. Thread the prawns onto the skewers, ensuring they are evenly spaced.
3. Brush the prawns generously with the garlic and parsley mixture, coating them on all sides.
4. Place the prawn skewers in Zone 1 of the air fryer. Select Zone 1, select the AIR FRY function, set temperature to 200°C and the cooking time to 10 minutes. Press the START/STOP button to begin cooking.
5. Halfway through the cooking process, carefully flip the skewers to ensure even cooking and browning.
6. Once the prawns are cooked through and the coating is crispy and golden, remove the skewers from the air fryer.
7. Lightly spray the prawns with vegetable oil spray for added crispiness, if desired.
8. Serve the **Prawn Dejonghe Skewers** as an appetizer or main dish, accompanied by a side of lemon wedges and your favorite dipping sauce.
9. Enjoy the succulent prawns with the flavorful garlic and parsley coating!

FOR BUTTER-WINE BAKED SALMON | SERVES 4

Prep time: 15 min | Cook time: 20 min

- 4 salmon fillets (about 150g each)
- 4 tablespoons unsalted butter, melted
- 3 tablespoons white wine
- 2 cloves garlic, minced
- 2 tablespoons fresh lemon juice
- 1 tablespoon chopped fresh dill
- Salt and pepper to taste
- Lemon slices and fresh dill sprigs for garnish.

DIRECTIONS:

1. In a small bowl, mix together the melted butter, white wine, minced garlic, fresh lemon juice, chopped dill, salt, and pepper.
2. Place the salmon fillets in a shallow baking dish or foil-lined tray.
3. Pour the butter-wine mixture over the salmon fillets, ensuring they are evenly coated.
4. Place the baking dish or tray with the salmon fillets in Zone 1 of the air fryer. Select Zone 1, select the AIR FRY function, set temperature to 180°C and set the cooking time to 15 minutes. Press the START/STOP button to begin cooking.
5. Halfway through the cooking process, baste the salmon fillets with the butter-wine mixture to keep them moist and flavorful.
6. Continue cooking until the salmon is cooked through and flakes easily with a fork.
7. Once done, carefully remove the salmon fillets from the air fryer and transfer them to a serving platter.
8. Garnish with fresh dill sprigs and lemon slices.
9. Serve the **Butter-Wine Baked Salmon** with your choice of sides, such as roasted vegetables or a fresh salad.
10. Enjoy the succulent and flavorful salmon!

PAPRIKA PRAWNS | SERVES 2

Prep time: 10 min | Cook time: 10 min

- 300g large prawns, peeled and deveined.
- 2 tablespoons olive oil
- 1 teaspoon smoked paprika
- 1/2 teaspoon garlic powder
- 1/4 teaspoon cayenne pepper (optional, for added heat)
- 1/2 teaspoon salt
- 1/4 teaspoon black pepper
- Fresh lemon wedges, for serving
- Chopped parsley, for garnish.

DIRECTIONS:

1. Preheat Zone 1 air fryer to the AIR FRY program at 200°C.
2. In a bowl, combine the olive oil, smoked paprika, garlic powder, cayenne pepper (if using), salt, and black pepper. Mix well.
3. Add the prawns to the bowl and toss until they are coated evenly with the spice mixture.
4. Place the prawns in Zone 1 of the air fryer. Select Zone 1, select the AIR FRY function, setting the temperature to 200°C and set the cooking time to 10 minutes. Press the START/STOP button to begin cooking.
5. Halfway through the cooking process, shake the air fryer basket to ensure even cooking.
6. Once the prawns are cooked and turn pink, remove them from the air fryer and transfer to a serving dish.
7. Squeeze fresh lemon juice over the prawns and garnish with chopped parsley.
8. Serve the Paprika Prawns as an appetizer or main dish with your favorite dipping sauce or alongside a fresh salad or rice.
9. Enjoy the delicious and flavorful **Paprika Prawns!**

ROASTED COD WITH LEMON-GARLIC POTATOES | SERVES 2

Prep time: 15 min | Cook time: 20 min

- 2 cod fillets (about 150g each)
- 300g baby potatoes, halved
- 2 tablespoons olive oil
- 2 cloves garlic, minced
- 1 lemon, zest and juice
- 1 teaspoon dried thyme
- Salt and pepper, to taste
- Chopped fresh parsley, for garnish

DIRECTIONS:

1. In a bowl, combine the olive oil, minced garlic, lemon zest, lemon juice, dried thyme, salt, and pepper. Mix well.
2. Add the halved baby potatoes to the bowl and toss until they are coated evenly with the marinade.
3. Place the marinated potatoes in Zone 1 of the air fryer. Select Zone 1, select the ROAST function, set temperature to 200°C and the cooking time to 15 minutes. Press the START/STOP button to begin roasting the potatoes.
4. While the potatoes are roasting, season the cod fillets with salt and pepper on both sides.
5. Place the seasoned cod fillets to Zone 2 of the air fryer. Select Zone 2, select the ROAST function, set temperature to 200°C and set the cooking time to 10 minutes. Press the START/STOP button to begin roasting the cod fillets.
6. Halfway through the cooking process, flip the cod fillets to ensure even cooking.
7. Once the potatoes are golden and crispy, and the cod fillets are cooked through and flaky, remove them from the air fryer.
8. Serve the roasted cod fillets on a plate alongside the lemon-garlic potatoes. Garnish with chopped fresh parsley.
9. Enjoy the delicious and satisfying **Roasted Cod with Lemon-Garlic Potatoes!**

SALMON ON BED OF FENNEL AND CARROT | SERVES 2

Prep time: 15 min | Cook time: 20 min

- 2 salmon fillets (about 150g each)
- 1 fennel bulb, thinly sliced
- 2 carrots, julienned
- 2 tablespoons olive oil
- 2 cloves garlic, minced
- 1 lemon, zest and juice
- 1 teaspoon dried dill
- Salt and pepper, to taste
- Chopped fresh dill, for garnish.

DIRECTIONS:

1. In Zone 1, place the thinly sliced fennel and julienned carrots. Drizzle with olive oil and sprinkle with minced garlic, dried dill, salt, and pepper. Toss to coat the vegetables evenly.
2. Select Zone 1, select the ROAST function, setting the temperature to 200°C and set the cooking time to 15 minutes. Press the START/STOP button to begin roasting the vegetables.
3. While the vegetables are roasting, season the salmon fillets with salt, pepper, and lemon zest on both sides.
4. Place the seasoned salmon fillets in Zone 2 of the air fryer. Select Zone 2, select the ROAST function, setting the temperature to 200°C and set the cooking time to 10 minutes. Press the START/STOP button to begin roasting the salmon fillets.
5. Halfway through the cooking process, drizzle the salmon fillets with lemon juice for added flavor.
6. Once the vegetables are tender and the salmon fillets are cooked through and flaky, remove them from the air fryer.
7. Serve the roasted salmon fillets on a plate on top of the bed of roasted fennel and carrot. Garnish with chopped fresh dill.
8. Enjoy the delightful and healthy **Salmon on Bed of Fennel and Carrot.**

GARLIC LEMON SCALLOPS | SERVES 4

Prep time: 10 min | Cook time: 10 min

- 500g scallops
- 2 tablespoons butter, melted
- 2 cloves garlic, minced
- Zest of 1 lemon
- Juice of 1 lemon
- 2 tablespoons chopped fresh parsley
- Salt and pepper, to taste
- Lemon wedges, for serving.

DIRECTIONS:

1. In a bowl, combine the melted butter, minced garlic, lemon zest, lemon juice, chopped parsley, salt, and pepper.
2. Pat dry the scallops with a paper towel to remove excess moisture.
3. Place the scallops in Zone 1 of the air fryer.
4. Drizzle the butter mixture over the scallops, ensuring they are evenly coated.
5. Select Zone 1, select the AIR FRY function, setting the temperature to 200°C and set the cooking time to 10 minutes. Press the START/STOP button to begin cooking the scallops.
6. Halfway through the cooking process, gently flip the scallops to ensure even browning.
7. Once the scallops are golden brown and cooked through, remove them from the air fryer.
8. Serve the Garlic Lemon Scallops on a platter, garnished with fresh parsley and accompanied by lemon wedges.
9. Enjoy the delicious and flavorful **Garlic Lemon Scallops!**

NUTTY PRAWNS WITH AMARETTO GLAZE | SERVES 10 TO 12

Prep time: 15 min | Cook time: 10 min

- 1 kg prawns, peeled and deveined
- 100 g breadcrumbs
- 50 g finely chopped mixed nuts (such as almonds, walnuts, and cashews)
- 25 g grated Parmesan cheese
- 2 tablespoons fresh parsley, chopped
- 2 tablespoons olive oil
- 2 tablespoons Amaretto liqueur
- 1 tablespoon lemon juice
- 2 cloves garlic, minced
- Salt and pepper, to taste
- Lemon wedges, for serving.

DIRECTIONS:

1. In a shallow bowl, combine the breadcrumbs, mixed nuts, Parmesan cheese, and chopped parsley.
2. In another bowl, whisk together the olive oil, Amaretto liqueur, lemon juice, minced garlic, salt, and pepper.
3. Dip each prawn into the olive oil mixture, allowing any excess to drip off.
4. Coat the prawns in the breadcrumb and nut mixture, pressing gently to adhere.
5. Place the coated prawns in both zone of the air fryer.
6. Select zone 1, select AIR FRY and set temperature to 200°C and set time to 10 minutes. Select MATCH to duplicate settings across both zones. Press the START/STOP button to begin cooking.
7. Halfway through the cooking process, gently shake the basket to ensure even cooking of the prawns.
8. Once the prawns are golden brown and cooked through, remove them from the air fryer.
9. Serve the **Nutty Prawns with Amaretto Glaze** on a platter, accompanied by lemon wedges for squeezing over the prawns.
10. Enjoy the delightful combination of crunchy nutty coating and the sweet Amaretto glaze on the succulent prawns!

CRAB-STUFFED AVOCADO BOATS | SERVES 4

Prep time: 15 min | Cook time: 8 min

- 2 ripe avocados
- 200g crabmeat
- 2 tablespoons mayonnaise
- 1 tablespoon lemon juice
- 2 tablespoons chopped fresh parsley
- 2 tablespoons chopped fresh chives
- 1/4 teaspoon garlic powder
- Salt and pepper, to taste
- Lemon wedges, for serving.

DIRECTIONS:

1. Cut the avocados in half lengthwise and remove the pits. Scoop out a little bit of flesh from each half to create a cavity for the stuffing. Chop the scooped-out avocado and set aside.
2. In a bowl, combine the crabmeat, mayonnaise, lemon juice, chopped parsley, chopped chives, garlic powder, salt, and pepper. Mix well.
3. Gently fold in the chopped avocado into the crab mixture.
4. Spoon the crab mixture into the hollowed-out avocado halves, mounding it up.
5. Place the stuffed avocado halves in Zone 1 of the air fryer.
6. Select Zone 1, select the AIR FRY function, set temperature to 180°C and set the cooking time to 8 minutes. Press the START/STOP button to begin cooking.
7. Once the cooking is complete, remove the Crab-Stuffed Avocado Boats from the air fryer.
8. Serve the avocado boats on a platter, garnished with additional chopped parsley and lemon wedges on the side.
9. Enjoy the creamy and flavorful **Crab-Stuffed Avocado Boats**!
10. Please note that the cooking times may vary depending on the size and ripeness of the avocados. Adjust the cooking time accordingly to achieve the desired level of doneness.

GARLIC BUTTER PRAWNS SCAMPI | SERVES 4

Prep time: 10 min | Cook time: 10 min

- 500g large prawns, peeled and deveined
- 4 tablespoons unsalted butter, melted
- 4 cloves garlic, minced
- 2 tablespoons chopped fresh parsley
- 1 tablespoon lemon juice
- Salt and pepper, to taste
- Lemon wedges, for serving.

DIRECTIONS:

1. In a bowl, combine the melted butter, minced garlic, chopped parsley, lemon juice, salt, and pepper. Mix well.
2. Add the peeled and deveined prawns to the bowl and toss to coat them evenly with the garlic butter mixture.
3. Place the prawns in Zone 1 of the air fryer in a single layer.
4. Select Zone 1, select the AIR FRY function, setting the temperature to 200°C and set the cooking time to 10 minutes. Press the START/STOP button to begin cooking.
5. Halfway through the cooking time, gently shake or flip the prawns to ensure even cooking.
6. Once the cooking is complete, remove the Garlic Butter Prawns Scampi from the air fryer.
7. Serve the prawns on a platter, garnished with additional chopped parsley and lemon wedges on the side.
8. Enjoy the succulent and flavorful **Garlic Butter Prawns Scampi**.
9. Note: Cooking times may vary depending on the size and thickness of the prawns. Adjust the cooking time accordingly to ensure they are cooked through and opaque.

MOROCCAN SPICED HALIBUT WITH CHICKPEA SALAD | SERVES 2

Prep time: 15 min | Cook time: 15 min

- 2 halibut fillets (about 150g each)
- 1 teaspoon ground cumin
- 1 teaspoon ground coriander
- 1/2 teaspoon ground paprika
- 1/2 teaspoon ground cinnamon
- 1/4 teaspoon cayenne pepper (adjust to taste)
- Salt and pepper, to taste
- 2 tablespoons olive oil

For the Chickpea Salad:
- 200g canned chickpeas, drained and rinsed
- 1/2 red onion, finely chopped
- 1/2 cucumber, diced
- 1 large tomato, diced
- 4 tablespoons chopped fresh parsley
- 1 tablespoon lemon juice
- 1 tablespoon extra-virgin olive oil
- Salt and pepper, to taste.

DIRECTIONS:

1. In a small bowl, mix together the ground cumin, ground coriander, ground paprika, ground cinnamon, cayenne pepper, salt, and pepper.
2. Rub the spice mixture all over the halibut fillets.
3. Place the seasoned halibut fillets in Zone 1 of the air fryer.
4. Select Zone 1, select the AIR FRY function, temperature to 200°C and set the cooking time to 15 minutes. Press the START/STOP button to begin cooking.
5. In the meantime, prepare the chickpea salad. In a mixing bowl, combine the drained and rinsed chickpeas, chopped red onion, diced cucumber, diced tomato, chopped parsley, lemon juice, extra-virgin olive oil, salt, and pepper. Mix well.
6. Once the cooking is complete, remove the halibut fillets from the air fryer. They should be flaky and cooked through.
7. Serve the Moroccan Spiced Halibut on a plate, accompanied by a generous serving of the chickpea salad.
8. Enjoy the delightful flavors of the **Moroccan Spiced Halibut with Chickpea Salad!**

COOKED TUNA WITH LEMONGRASS | SERVES 4

Prep time: 15 min | Cook time: 12 min

- 4 tuna steaks
- 2 stalks lemongrass, white part only, finely chopped
- 2 cloves garlic, minced
- 2 tablespoons soy sauce
- 1 tablespoon fish sauce
- 1 tablespoon lime juice
- 1 tablespoon vegetable oil
- Salt and pepper to taste
- Fresh cilantro for garnish (optional)

DIRECTIONS:

1. In a bowl, combine the chopped lemongrass, minced garlic, soy sauce, fish sauce, lime juice, vegetable oil, salt, and pepper. Mix well to create the marinade.
2. Place the tuna steaks in a shallow dish and0 pour the marinade over them. Make sure the tuna steaks are coated evenly. Allow them to marinate for at least 10 minutes.
3. Then place marinated tuna steaks in zone 1.
4. Select Zone 1, select the AIR FRY function, temperature to 200°C and set the cooking time to 12 minutes. Press the START/STOP button to begin cooking
5. Cook the tuna steaks for about 5-6 minutes per side, or until desired doneness. The internal temperature should reach 54-57°C for medium-rare.
6. Once cooked, remove the tuna steaks from the heat and let them rest for a few minutes.
7. Serve the **Cooked Tuna with Lemongrass** hot, garnished with fresh cilantro if desired. They pair well with steamed rice or a fresh salad.

MISO SALMON I SERVES 2

Prep time: 15 min | Cook time: 10 min

- 2 salmon fillets
- 2 tablespoons white miso paste
- 1 tablespoon honey
- 1 tablespoon soy sauce
- 1 tablespoon rice vinegar
- 1 teaspoon grated fresh ginger
- 1 clove garlic, minced
- 1 tablespoon vegetable oil
- Sesame seeds, for garnish
- Sliced spring onions, for garnish.

DIRECTIONS:

1. In a small bowl, whisk together the miso paste, honey, soy sauce, rice vinegar, grated ginger, minced garlic, and vegetable oil to make the marinade.
2. Place the salmon fillets in a shallow dish or a resealable plastic bag. Pour the marinade over the salmon, ensuring it is well-coated. Let it marinate for about 10 minutes.
3. Remove the salmon fillets from the marinade, reserving the marinade for later use.
4. Place the salmon fillets on the grill grate or in the cooking basket of Zone 1.
5. Select Zone 1, select the AIR FRY function, temperature to 200°C and set the cooking time to 10 minutes. Press the START/STOP button to begin cooking.
6. While the salmon is cooking, transfer the reserved marinade to a small saucepan. Bring it to a boil over medium heat, then reduce the heat and simmer for a few minutes until it thickens slightly.
7. Once the salmon is cooked and flakes easily with a fork, remove it from the air fryer.
8. Drizzle the cooked salmon with the thickened marinade.
9. Garnish with sesame seeds and sliced spring onions.
10. Serve the **Miso Salmon** hot with steamed rice or a side of vegetables.

Note: Adjust the cooking time based on the thickness of the salmon fillets

THAI PRAWN SKEWERS WITH PEANUT DIPPING SAUCE | SERVES 2

Prep time: 20 min | Cook time: 10 min

For the Prawn Skewers:
- 12 large prawns, peeled and deveined
- 2 tablespoons soy sauce
- 2 tablespoons fish sauce
- 2 tablespoons lime juice
- 1 tablespoon honey
- 1 tablespoon vegetable oil
- 2 cloves garlic, minced
- 1 tablespoon fresh coriander, chopped
- 1 red chili, seeded and finely chopped (optional)
- Bamboo skewers, soaked in water for 30 minutes.

For the Peanut Dipping Sauce:
- 3 tablespoons peanut butter
- 2 tablespoons soy sauce
- 1 tablespoon lime juice
- 1 tablespoon honey
- 1 teaspoon sesame oil
- Water (as needed to adjust consistency)
- Crushed peanuts, for garnish (optional)
- Fresh coriander, for garnish (optional)

DIRECTIONS

1. In a bowl, combine the soy sauce, fish sauce, lime juice, honey, vegetable oil, minced garlic, chopped coriander, and chopped red chili (if using). Mix well to make the marinade.
2. Add the prawns to the marinade and toss to coat them evenly. Allow the prawns to marinate for at least 15 minutes.
3. Thread the marinated prawns onto the soaked bamboo skewers.
4. Place the prawn skewers on the grill grate or in the cooking basket of Zone 1.
5. Select Zone 1, select the AIR FRY function, set the temperature to 180°C and set the cooking time to 10 minutes . Press the START/STOP button to begin cooking.
6. While the prawns are cooking, prepare the peanut dipping sauce. In a separate bowl, whisk together the peanut butter, soy sauce, lime juice, honey, and sesame oil. Add water gradually to achieve the desired consistency for dipping.
7. Once the prawns are cooked and have turned pink, remove them from the air fryer.
8. Serve the **Thai prawn skewers with the peanut dipping sauce** on the side.
9. Garnish with crushed peanuts and fresh coriander, if desired.
10. Note: Adjust the cooking time based on the size and thickness of the prawns. Ensure that the prawns are cooked through and opaque.

FOIL-PACKET LOBSTER TAIL | SERVES 2

Prep time: 10 min | Cook time: 12 min

- 2 lobster tails
- 2 tablespoons unsalted butter, melted
- 2 cloves garlic, minced
- 1 tablespoon fresh lemon juice
- Salt and pepper, to taste
- Fresh parsley, chopped (for garnish)
- Lemon wedges (for serving)

DIRECTIONS:

1. Preheat the Zone 1 to the AIR FRY function at 200°C in 3 minutes.
2. Using kitchen shears, carefully cut through the top shell of each lobster tail lengthwise, stopping before the tail fins.
3. Gently lift the lobster meat from the shell, keeping it attached at the base, and place it on top of the shell.
4. In a small bowl, combine the melted butter, minced garlic, and lemon juice. Season with salt and pepper to taste.
5. Brush the garlic butter mixture generously over each lobster tail, making sure to coat all exposed meat.
6. Place each lobster tail on a separate piece of foil. Fold up the edges of the foil to create a packet, leaving a small vent on top to allow steam to escape.
7. Place the foil packets with the lobster tails in Zone 1 of the Ninja Dual Zone air fryer.
8. Select Zone 1, select the AIR FRY function, set temperature to 200°C and set the cooking time to 12 minutes . Press the START/STOP button to begin cooking.
9. While the lobster tails are cooking, you can prepare any side dishes or sauces to accompany the meal.
10. Once the cooking time is complete, carefully open the foil packets (watch out for steam) and transfer the lobster tails to serving plates.
11. Garnish with freshly chopped parsley and serve with lemon wedges on the side.
12. Enjoy the **Foil-Packet Lobster Tails** while they're hot and tender!

SCALLOPS WITH ASPARAGUS AND PEAS I SERVES 4

Prep time: 10 min | Cook time: 10 min

- 16 large scallops
- 200g asparagus spears, trimmed
- 200g fresh or frozen peas
- 2 tablespoons olive oil
- 2 cloves garlic, minced
- 1 lemon, zest and juice
- Salt and pepper, to taste
- Fresh parsley, for garnish

DIRECTIONS:

1. In a mixing bowl, combine the asparagus spears, peas, olive oil, minced garlic, lemon zest, salt, and pepper. Toss to coat the vegetables evenly.
2. Once the air fryer is preheated, place the seasoned vegetables in Zone 1 and arrange the scallops in Zone 2 of the air fryer.
3. Select zone 1, select AIR FRY and set temperature to 200°C and set time to 10 minutes. Select MATCH to duplicate settings across both zones. Press the START/STOP button to begin cooking.
4. Cook for 5 minutes, then carefully flip the scallops and stir the vegetables.
5. Continue cooking for another 5 minutes or until the scallops are opaque and cooked through, and the vegetables are tender-crisp.
6. Once cooked, remove the scallops and vegetables from the air fryer. Squeeze fresh lemon juice over the scallops and vegetables.
7. Serve the **scallops on a plate with the asparagus and pea** mixture. Garnish with fresh parsley.

BREADED PRAWNS TACOS | MAKES 8 TACOS

Prep time: 20 min | Cook time: 10 min

- 300g prawns, peeled and deveined
- 100g all-purpose flour
- 2 eggs, beaten
- 100g breadcrumbs
- 1 teaspoon paprika
- 1/2 teaspoon garlic powder
- 1/2 teaspoon salt
- 1/4 teaspoon black pepper
- 8 small flour tortillas.

- 50 grams shredded lettuce
- 75 grams diced tomatoes
- 30 grams diced red onion
- Fresh cilantro leaves (for garnish)
- Lime wedges (for serving)
- Your choice of sauce (such as tartar sauce or chili sauce)

DIRECTIONS

1. In three separate shallow bowls or plates, set up your breading station. In the first bowl, place the all-purpose flour. In the second bowl, beat the eggs. In the third bowl, combine the breadcrumbs, paprika, garlic powder, salt, and black pepper.
2. Take a prawn and dip it into the flour, coating it lightly. Shake off any excess flour.
3. Dip the floured prawn into the beaten eggs, ensuring it is coated evenly.
4. Transfer the prawn to the breadcrumb mixture and coat it well, pressing gently to adhere the breadcrumbs to the prawn. Repeat this process with the remaining prawns.
5. Lightly grease the cooking basket in Zone 1 of the Ninja Dual Zone Air Fryer with cooking spray or brush it with a small amount of oil.
6. Arrange the breaded prawns in a single layer in Zone 1's cooking basket. (If there are still breaded prawns, place them to zone 2)
7. Select Zone 1, choose the AIR FRY function, and set the temperature to 200°C. Set the cooking time to 10 minutes. (if place breaded prawns in both zone , Select MATCH). Press the START/STOP button to begin cooking.
8. While the prawns are cooking, warm the flour tortillas according to package instructions.
9. Once the prawns are cooked and golden brown, carefully remove them from the air fryer.
10. To assemble the tacos, place a tortilla on a flat surface. Add a layer of shredded lettuce, followed by a few breaded prawns. Top with diced tomatoes, diced red onion, and fresh cilantro leaves.
11. Serve the Breaded Prawns Tacos with lime wedges and your choice of sauce on the side.
12. Enjoy the delicious **Breaded Prawns Tacos** while they're still warm and crispy!

BROWNED PRAWNS PATTIES | SERVES 4

Prep time: 20 min | Cook time: 12 min

- 500g (1.1 lbs) prawns, peeled and deveined
- 1 small onion, finely chopped
- 2 cloves garlic, minced
- 25g breadcrumbs
- 2 tablespoons mayonnaise
- 1 tablespoon Worcestershire sauce
- 1 tablespoon Dijon mustard
- 1 tablespoon chopped fresh parsley
- 1/2 teaspoon salt
- 1/4 teaspoon black pepper
- 2 tablespoons vegetable oil.

DIRECTIONS:

1. Select Zone 1 on the Ninja Dual Zone Air Fryer and preheat it to 200°C for 3 minutes.
2. In a food processor, add the prawns and pulse until coarsely chopped. Transfer the chopped prawns to a mixing bowl.
3. To the bowl with the prawns, add the chopped onion, minced garlic, breadcrumbs, mayonnaise, Worcestershire sauce, Dijon mustard, chopped fresh parsley, salt, and black pepper. Mix well to combine all the ingredients.
4. Form the mixture into patties, approximately 8 patties of equal size.
5. Once Zone 1 is preheated, lightly brush the air fryer basket in Zone 1 with vegetable oil. Place the prawn patties in Zone 1's cooking basket in a single layer.
6. Select Zone 1, choosing AIR FRY, set the temperature to 200°C, and set the cooking time to 10-12 minutes. Press the START/STOP button to begin cooking.
7. While the patties are cooking, you can prepare a sauce or a side salad to accompany the prawn patties.
8. After the cooking time is complete, carefully remove the browned prawn patties from the air fryer.
9. Serve the **Browned Prawn Patties** hot, either on their own or in burger buns with your preferred condiments.

LEMON PEPPER PRAWNS | SERVES 2

Prep time: 15 min | Cook time: 10 min

- 300g (10.5oz) large prawns, peeled and deveined
- 2 tablespoons olive oil
- 1 lemon (zest and juice)
- 1 teaspoon ground black pepper
- 1/2 teaspoon salt
- 1 teaspoon dried parsley
- 1/2 teaspoon garlic powder
- Optional: Fresh parsley, chopped (for garnish)

DIRECTIONS:

1. Select Zone 1 on the Ninja Dual Zone Air Fryer and preheat it to 200°C for 3 minutes.
2. In a bowl, combine the olive oil, lemon zest, lemon juice, black pepper, salt, dried parsley, and garlic powder. Mix well to create a marinade.
3. Add the prawns to the marinade and toss them to coat evenly. Allow the prawns to marinate for 10 minutes.
4. Once Zone 1 is preheated, place the marinated prawns in Zone 1's cooking basket in a single layer.
5. Select Zone 1, choosing AIR FRY, set the temperature to 200°C and set the cooking time to 10 minutes. Press the START/STOP button to begin cooking.
6. While the prawns are cooking, you can prepare a side salad or your preferred accompaniment.
7. After the cooking time is complete, carefully remove the cooked prawns from the air fryer.
8. Serve the Lemon Pepper Prawns immediately. You can garnish them with fresh chopped parsley, if desired.
9. Enjoy the flavorful and succulent **Lemon Pepper Prawns**!

Chapter 8: Snacks and Appetizers

BAKED SPANAKOPITA DIP | SERVES 2

Prep time: 15 min | Cook time: 20 min

- 200g frozen spinach, thawed and drained
- 100g feta cheese, crumbled
- 50g cream cheese
- 25g grated Parmesan cheese
- 2 cloves garlic, minced
- 1/2 teaspoon dried dill
- 1/4 teaspoon salt
- 1/4 teaspoon black pepper
- 2 tablespoons olive oil

DIRECTIONS:

1. Preheat the Ninja Dual Zone Air Fryer to the "Bake" program at the recommended temperature for baking (usually around 180°C/350°F). Preheat for a few minutes to ensure it reaches the desired temperature.
2. In a mixing bowl, combine the thawed and drained spinach, crumbled feta cheese, cream cheese, grated Parmesan cheese, minced garlic, dried dill, salt, black pepper, and olive oil. Mix well to combine all the ingredients.
3. Transfer the mixture to an oven-safe baking dish that fits inside the air fryer basket.
4. Place the baking dish in the air fryer basket in the Zone 1 cooking area.
5. Select zone 1, select BAKE and set temperature to 180°C and set time to 16-20 minutes. Press the START/STOP button to begin cooking.
6. Once the cooking time is complete, carefully remove the baking dish from the air fryer using oven mitts or heat-resistant gloves.
7. Serve the **Baked Spanakopita Dip** hot, alongside pita bread, tortilla chips, or your preferred dipping accompaniment.

PARMESAN FRENCH FRIES | SERVES 2

Prep time: 10 min | Cook time: 20 min

- 4 medium-sized potatoes
- 2 tablespoons olive oil
- 25g grated Parmesan cheese
- 1 teaspoon garlic powder
- 1/2 teaspoon paprika
- 1/2 teaspoon dried thyme
- 1/2 teaspoon salt
- 1/4 teaspoon black pepper
- Fresh parsley, chopped (for garnish)

DIRECTIONS:

1. Wash and peel the potatoes. Cut them into thin, evenly-sized French fry shapes.
2. In a large bowl, toss the potato fries with olive oil until they are evenly coated.
3. In a separate bowl, combine the grated Parmesan cheese, garlic powder, paprika, dried thyme, salt, and black pepper.
4. Sprinkle the Parmesan cheese mixture over the oiled potato fries and toss until the fries are well-coated with the seasoning.
5. Lightly grease the cooking basket in two zone of the Ninja Dual Zone Air Fryer with cooking spray or brush it with a small amount of oil.
6. Arrange the seasoned potato fries in a single layer in both zone cooking basket.
7. Select Zone 1, choose the AIR FRY function, and set the temperature to 200°C. Set the cooking time to 18-22 minutes. Select MATCH. Press the START/STOP button to begin cooking.
8. Halfway through the cooking time, pause the air fryer and shake the baskets to ensure even cooking. Then, continue cooking until the fries are crispy and golden brown.
9. Once the cooking time is complete, carefully remove the basket from the air fryer.
10. Sprinkle the **Parmesan French Fries** with fresh chopped parsley for added freshness and flavor. Serve immediately as a delicious side dish or snack.

PICKLE CHIPS | SERVES 4

Prep time: 15 min | Cook time: 10 min

- 400g dill pickle chips (sliced pickles)
- 100g all-purpose flour
- 2 large eggs, beaten
- 100g breadcrumbs
- 1 teaspoon paprika
- 1/2 teaspoon garlic powder
- 1/2 teaspoon dried dill
- 1/2 teaspoon salt
- 1/4 teaspoon black pepper
- Cooking spray or oil for greasing.

DIRECTIONS:

1. Pat dry the pickle chips using a paper towel to remove excess moisture.
2. Set up a breading station: In one bowl, place the all-purpose flour. In another bowl, beat the eggs. In a third bowl, combine the breadcrumbs, paprika, garlic powder, dried dill, salt, and black pepper.
3. Take a pickle chip and dip it into the flour, coating it lightly. Shake off any excess flour.
4. Dip the floured pickle chip into the beaten eggs, ensuring it is coated evenly.
5. Transfer the pickle chip to the breadcrumb mixture and coat it well, pressing gently to adhere the breadcrumbs to the pickle chip. Repeat this process with the remaining pickle chips.
6. Lightly grease the cooking basket in both zone of the Ninja Dual Zone Air Fryer with cooking spray or brush it with a small amount of oil.
7. Arrange the breaded pickle chips in a single layer in two zone s cooking basket.
8. Select Zone 1, choose the AIR FRY function, and set the temperature to 200°C. Set the cooking time to 8-10 minutes. Select MATCH. Press the START/STOP button to begin cooking.
9. Halfway through the cooking time, pause the air fryer and shake the baskets to ensure even cooking. Then, continue cooking until the pickle chips are golden brown and crispy.
10. Once the cooking time is complete, carefully remove the basket from the air fryer.
11. Serve the **Pickle Chips** immediately as a delicious appetizer or snack

SWEET POTATO FRIES WITH MAYONNAISE | SERVES 2

Prep time: 10 min | Cook time: 20 min

- 2 medium-sized sweet potatoes
- 2 tablespoons cornstarch
- 1 tablespoon olive oil
- 1/2 teaspoon paprika
- 1/2 teaspoon garlic powder
- 1/2 teaspoon salt
- 1/4 teaspoon black pepper
- Cooking spray or oil for greasing
- Mayonnaise, for serving.

DIRECTIONS:

1. Wash and peel the sweet potatoes. Cut them into thin, even-sized strips to resemble fries.
2. In a large bowl, combine the cornstarch, paprika, garlic powder, salt, and black pepper. Toss the sweet potato fries in the cornstarch mixture until they are evenly coated.
3. Drizzle the olive oil over the coated sweet potato fries and toss to ensure the fries are well-coated.
4. Lightly grease the cooking basket in Zone 1 of the Ninja Dual Zone Air Fryer with cooking spray or brush it with a small amount of oil.
5. Arrange the sweet potato fries in a single layer in Zone 1 cooking basket.
6. Select Zone 1, choose the AIR FRY function, and set the temperature to 200°C. Set the cooking time to 20 minutes. Press the START/STOP button to begin cooking.
7. Halfway through the cooking time, pause the air fryer and shake the basket to ensure even cooking. Then, continue cooking until the sweet potato fries are crispy and golden brown.
8. Once the cooking time is complete, carefully remove the basket from the air fryer.
9. Serve the **Sweet Potato Fries** immediately with a side of mayonnaise for dipping.

AIR FRIED POT STICKERS | MAKES 30 POT STICKERS

Prep time: 30 min | Cook time: 10 min

- 30 round dumpling wrappers
- 300g ground pork
- 100g cabbage, finely chopped
- 50g spring onions, finely chopped
- 1 tablespoon soy sauce
- 1 tablespoon sesame oil
- 1/2 teaspoon grated ginger
- 1/2 teaspoon garlic powder
- 1/4 teaspoon black pepper
- Water, for sealing the pot stickers
- Soy sauce and vinegar, for dipping

DIRECTIONS:

1. In a large bowl, combine the ground pork, chopped cabbage, chopped spring onions, soy sauce, sesame oil, grated ginger, garlic powder, and black pepper. Mix well until all the ingredients are evenly incorporated.
2. Place a dumpling wrapper on a clean surface. Spoon about 1 tablespoon of the pork mixture onto the center of the wrapper.
3. Dip your finger into water and run it along the edge of the dumpling wrapper. Fold the wrapper in half, creating a half-moon shape, and press the edges firmly to seal the pot sticker. Repeat this process with the remaining wrappers and filling.
4. Lightly grease the cooking basket in Zone 1 with cooking spray or brush it with a small amount of oil.
5. Arrange the pot stickers in a single layer in Zone 1's cooking basket, ensuring they are not touching each other. (if there are leftovers, put them in zone 2 and cook on both zones)
6. Select Zone 1, choose the AIR FRY function, and set the temperature to 190°C. Set the cooking time to 10 minutes. Press the START/STOP.
7. Once the cooking time is complete, carefully remove the basket from the air fryer.
8. Serve the **Air Fried Pot Stickers** immediately with a dipping sauce made from soy sauce and vinegar.

CRISPY MOZZARELLA STICKS | SERVES 4

Prep time: 15 min | Cook time: 10 min

- 200g mozzarella cheese, cut into sticks
- 100g all-purpose flour
- 2 large eggs, beaten
- 100g breadcrumbs
- 1 teaspoon dried oregano
- 1/2 teaspoon garlic powder
- 1/2 teaspoon paprika
- 1/4 teaspoon salt
- 1/4 teaspoon black pepper
- Cooking spray or oil for greasing
- Marinara sauce or any dipping sauce of your choice.

DIRECTIONS:

1. Set up a breading station: In one bowl, place the all-purpose flour. In another bowl, beat the eggs. In a third bowl, combine the breadcrumbs, dried oregano, garlic powder, paprika, salt, and black pepper.
2. Take a mozzarella stick and coat it in the flour, shaking off any excess.
3. Dip the floured mozzarella stick into the beaten eggs, ensuring it is coated evenly.
4. Transfer the mozzarella stick to the breadcrumb mixture and coat it well, pressing gently to adhere the breadcrumbs to the cheese. Repeat this process with the remaining mozzarella sticks.
5. Lightly grease the cooking basket in Zone 1 of the Ninja Dual Zone Air Fryer with cooking spray or brush it with a small amount of oil.
6. Arrange the breaded mozzarella sticks in a single layer in Zone 1's cooking basket.
7. Select Zone 1, choose the AIR FRY, set the temperature to 200°C. Set the cooking time to 8-10 minutes. Press the START/STOP.
8. Halfway through the cooking time, pause the air fryer and shake the basket to ensure even cooking. Then, continue cooking until the mozzarella sticks are golden brown and crispy.
9. Once the cooking time is complete, carefully remove the basket from the air fryer.
10. Serve **Crispy Mozzarella Sticks** immediately with marinara sauce or any dipping sauce of your choice.

CHILLI-BRINED FRIED CALAMARI | SERVES 2

Prep time: 70 min | Cook time: 10 min

- 250g calamari rings
- 480g buttermilk
- 1 tablespoon hot sauce
- 1 teaspoon paprika
- 1/2 teaspoon garlic powder
- 1/2 teaspoon salt
- 1/4 teaspoon black pepper
- 100g all-purpose flour
- Cooking spray or oil for greasing
- Lemon wedges, for serving.

DIRECTIONS:

1. In a bowl, combine the buttermilk, hot sauce, paprika, garlic powder, salt, and black pepper. Stir well to mix the ingredients.
2. Add the calamari rings to the buttermilk mixture, ensuring they are fully submerged. Cover the bowl and refrigerate for at least 1 hour to allow the calamari to marinate.
3. In a shallow dish, place the all-purpose flour.
4. Remove the marinated calamari rings from the buttermilk mixture, allowing any excess liquid to drip off.
5. Dredge the calamari rings in the flour, coating them evenly. Shake off any excess flour.
6. Lightly grease the cooking basket in Zone 1 of the Ninja Dual Zone Air Fryer with cooking spray or brush it with a small amount of oil.
7. Arrange the breaded calamari rings in a single layer in Zone 1's cooking basket. (if leftovers, put them in zone 2 and cook on both zones)
8. Select Zone 1, choose the AIR FRY function, and set the temperature to 200°C. Set the cooking time to 8-10 minutes. Press the START/STOP button to begin cooking.
9. Halfway through the cooking time, pause the air fryer and shake the basket to ensure even cooking. Then, continue cooking until the calamari rings are golden brown and crispy.
10. Once the cooking time is complete, carefully remove the basket from the air fryer.
11. Serve the **Chilli-Brined Fried Calamari** immediately with lemon wedges for squeezing over the calamari.

ROASTED GRAPE DIP | SERVES 6

Prep time: 10 min | Cook time: 15 min

- 500g seedless grapes
- 2 tablespoons olive oil
- 1 tablespoon honey
- 200g cream cheese, softened
- 200g Greek yogurt
- 1 teaspoon lemon juice
- 1/2 teaspoon dried thyme
- 1/4 teaspoon salt
- 1/4 teaspoon black pepper
- Crackers or bread, for serving.

DIRECTIONS:

1. Preheat the Ninja Dual Zone Air Fryer to 200°C in Zone 1 for a few minutes.
2. In a bowl, toss the grapes with olive oil and honey until they are well coated.
3. Lightly grease the cooking basket in Zone 1 of the Ninja Dual Zone Air Fryer with cooking spray or brush it with a small amount of oil.
4. Place the grape mixture in Zone 1's cooking basket in a single layer.
5. Select Zone 1, choose the ROAST function, and set the temperature to 200°C. Set the cooking time to 15 minutes. Press the START/STOP button to begin cooking.
6. While the grapes are roasting, in a separate bowl, combine the softened cream cheese, Greek yogurt, lemon juice, dried thyme, salt, and black pepper. Mix well until smooth and creamy.
7. Once the cooking time is complete, carefully remove the basket from the air fryer.
8. Allow the roasted grapes to cool slightly, then chop them into smaller pieces.
9. Add the chopped roasted grapes to the cream cheese mixture and stir until well combined.
10. Transfer the Roasted Grape Dip to a serving bowl. Serve the **Roasted Grape Dip** with crackers or bread.

CRISPY CHILLI CHICKPEAS | SERVES 4

Prep time: 5 min | Cook time: 15 min

- 2 cans (400g each) chickpeas, drained and rinsed
- 2 tablespoons olive oil
- 1 teaspoon smoked paprika
- 1/2 teaspoon ground cumin
- 1/2 teaspoon garlic powder
- 1/4 teaspoon cayenne pepper (adjust according to spice preference)
- 1/2 teaspoon salt
- 1/4 teaspoon black pepper
- Freshly squeezed lemon juice, for serving
- Chopped fresh cilantro, for garnish (optional)

DIRECTIONS:

1. Preheat the Ninja Dual Zone Air Fryer to 200°C in Zone 1 for a few minutes.
2. In a bowl, combine the chickpeas, olive oil, smoked paprika, ground cumin, garlic powder, cayenne pepper, salt, and black pepper. Toss well to coat the chickpeas evenly with the spices.
3. Lightly grease the cooking basket in Zone 1 of the Ninja Dual Zone Air Fryer with cooking spray or brush it with a small amount of oil.
4. Place the seasoned chickpeas in Zone 1's cooking basket in a single layer.
5. Select Zone 1, choose the AIR FRY function, and set the temperature to 200°C. Set the cooking time to 15 minutes. Press the START/STOP button to begin cooking.
6. Halfway through the cooking time, pause the air fryer and shake the basket to ensure even cooking. Then, continue cooking until the chickpeas are crispy and golden brown.
7. Once the cooking time is complete, carefully remove the basket from the air fryer.
8. Squeeze some fresh lemon juice over the crispy chickpeas for added tanginess.
9. Sprinkle with chopped fresh cilantro if desired. Serve the **Crispy Chilli Chickpeas** as a delicious and healthy snack.

TANGY FRIED PICKLE SPEARS | SERVES 6

Prep time: 15 min | Cook time: 10 min

- 400g dill pickle spears
- 65g all-purpose flour
- 80g cornmeal
- 1 teaspoon paprika
- 1/2 teaspoon garlic powder
- 1/4 teaspoon cayenne pepper (adjust according to spice preference)
- 1/2 teaspoon salt
- 1/4 teaspoon black pepper
- 2 large eggs
- 2 tablespoons milk
- Cooking spray or oil for greasing
- Ranch dressing or dipping sauce of your choice, for serving.

DIRECTIONS:

1. Preheat Zone 1 to 200°C for a few minutes.
2. In a shallow dish, combine the all-purpose flour, cornmeal, paprika, garlic powder, cayenne pepper, salt, and black pepper. Mix well.
3. In a separate bowl, whisk together the eggs and milk.
4. Lightly grease the cooking basket in Zone 1 of the Ninja Dual Zone Air Fryer with cooking spray or brush it with a small amount of oil.
5. Dip each pickle spear into the egg mixture, allowing any excess to drip off, then coat it with the flour mixture. Repeat for all pickle spears.
6. Place the breaded pickle spears in Zone 1's cooking basket in a single layer.
7. Select Zone 1, choose the AIR FRY function, and set the temperature to 200°C. Set the cooking time to 10 minutes. Press the START/STOP button to begin cooking.
8. Halfway through the cooking time, pause the air fryer and shake the basket to ensure even cooking. Then, continue cooking until the pickle spears are golden brown and crispy.
9. Once the cooking time is complete, carefully remove the basket from the air fryer.
10. Serve the **Tangy Fried Pickle Spears** hot with ranch dressing or your preferred dipping sauce.

CRISPY FILO ARTICHOKE TRIANGLES | MAKES 18 TRIANGLES

Prep time: 20 min | Cook time: 15 min

- 200g canned artichoke hearts, drained and chopped
- 100g feta cheese, crumbled
- 50g grated Parmesan cheese
- 2 tablespoons chopped fresh dill
- 2 tablespoons chopped fresh parsley
- 1 teaspoon lemon zest
- Salt and pepper to taste
- 9 sheets of filo pastry
- Butter or cooking spray for greasing.

DIRECTIONS

1. Preheat the Ninja Dual Zone Air Fryer to 200°C in both zone for a few minutes.
2. In a bowl, combine the chopped artichoke hearts, crumbled feta cheese, grated Parmesan cheese, chopped fresh dill, chopped fresh parsley, lemon zest, salt, and pepper. Mix well to combine the filling ingredients.
3. Lay one sheet of filo pastry on a clean work surface and brush it lightly with melted butter or spray it with cooking spray. Place another sheet of filo pastry on top and repeat the process until you have a stack of three filo sheets.
4. Cut the filo stack into six equal squares.
5. Place a spoonful of the artichoke filling onto each filo square. Fold the filo square diagonally to form a triangle, enclosing the filling. Press the edges firmly to seal.
6. Repeat the process with the remaining filo sheets and filling until you have 18 filled triangles.
7. Lightly grease the cooking basket in two zone of the Ninja Dual Zone Air Fryer with cooking spray or brush it with a small amount of melted butter.
8. Place the filo triangles in both zone cooking basket in a single layer.
9. Select Zone 1, choose the AIR FRY function, and set the temperature to 200°C. Set the cooking time to 15 minutes. Select MATCH. Press the START/STOP.
10. Halfway through the cooking time, pause the air fryer and flip the filo triangles to ensure even browning. Then, continue cooking until the triangles are golden brown and crispy.
11. Once the cooking time is complete, carefully remove the basket from the air fryer.
12. Serve the **Crispy Filo Artichoke Triangles** as a delicious appetizer or snack.

EASY SPICED NUTS | SERVES 4

Prep time: 5 min | Cook time: 10 min

- 200g mixed nuts (such as almonds, cashews, and walnuts)
- 1 tablespoon olive oil
- 1 tablespoon honey
- 1 teaspoon ground cinnamon
- 1/2 teaspoon ground cumin
- 1/4 teaspoon cayenne pepper (adjust according to spice preference)
- 1/2 teaspoon salt.

DIRECTIONS:

1. Preheat the Ninja Dual Zone Air Fryer to 180°C in Zone 1 for a few minutes
2. In a bowl, combine the mixed nuts, olive oil, honey, ground cinnamon, ground cumin, cayenne pepper, and salt. Toss well to coat the nuts evenly with the spice mixture.
3. Lightly grease the cooking basket in Zone 1 of the Ninja Dual Zone Air Fryer with cooking spray or a small amount of oil.
4. Place the spiced nuts in Zone 1's cooking basket in a single layer.
5. Select Zone 1, choose the AIR FRY function, and set the temperature to 180°C. Set the cooking time to 10 minutes. Press the START/STOP button to begin cooking.
6. Halfway through the cooking time, pause the air fryer and shake the basket to ensure even cooking. Then, continue cooking until the nuts are toasted and fragrant.
7. Once the cooking time is complete, carefully remove the basket from the air fryer.
8. Allow the spiced nuts to cool slightly before serving.
9. Serve the **Easy Spiced Nuts** as a tasty snack or appetizer.

CRISPY GREEN TOMATOES WITH HORSERADISH | SERVES 4

Prep time: 15 min | Cook time: 10 min

- 4 green tomatoes
- 70g all-purpose flour
- 2 large eggs
- 100g breadcrumbs
- 25g grated Parmesan cheese
- 1/2 teaspoon paprika
- 1/2 teaspoon garlic powder
- Salt and pepper to taste
- 4 tablespoons horseradish sauce

DIRECTIONS:

1. Preheat the Ninja Dual Zone Air Fryer to 200°C in Zone 1 for a few minutes.
2. Slice the green tomatoes into 1/4-inch thick rounds.
3. Place the flour in a shallow dish. In another shallow dish, whisk the eggs until well beaten. In a third shallow dish, combine the breadcrumbs, grated Parmesan cheese, paprika, garlic powder, salt, and pepper.
4. Dip each tomato slice into the flour, shaking off any excess. Then dip it into the beaten eggs, allowing any excess to drip off. Finally, coat the tomato slice in the breadcrumb mixture, pressing gently to adhere the coating.
5. Lightly grease the cooking basket in Zone 1 of the Ninja Dual Zone Air Fryer with cooking spray or a small amount of oil.
6. Place the coated tomato slices in Zone 1's cooking basket in a single layer.
7. Select Zone 1, choose the AIR FRY function, and set the temperature to 200°C. Set the cooking time to 10 minutes. Press the START/STOP button to begin cooking.
8. Halfway through the cooking time, pause the air fryer and flip the tomato slices to ensure even browning. Then, continue cooking until the tomatoes are crispy and golden brown.
9. Once the cooking time is complete, carefully remove the basket from the air fryer.
10. Serve the **Crispy Green Tomatoes** with a side of horseradish sauce for dipping.

VEGGIE SHRIMP TOAST | SERVES 4

Prep time: 20 min | Cook time: 10 min

- 200g cooked shrimp, peeled and chopped
- 1 small carrot, grated
- 1/2 small zucchini, grated
- 2 spring onions, finely chopped
- 2 tablespoons fresh cilantro, chopped
- 1 clove garlic, minced
- 1 teaspoon grated ginger
- 1 tablespoon soy sauce
- 1 teaspoon sesame oil
- 1/2 teaspoon salt
- 1/4 teaspoon black pepper
- 8 slices of bread
- Sesame seeds for garnish.

DIRECTIONS:

1. Preheat Zone 1 to 200°C in for a few minutes.
2. In a mixing bowl, combine the cooked shrimp, grated carrot, grated zucchini, chopped spring onions, fresh cilantro, minced garlic, grated ginger, soy sauce, sesame oil, salt, and black pepper. Mix well to combine all the ingredients.
3. Cut the slices of bread into quarters to form smaller triangles.
4. Spoon a generous amount of the shrimp and vegetable mixture onto each bread triangle, spreading it evenly.
5. Lightly grease the cooking basket in Zone 1 of the Ninja Dual Zone Air Fryer with cooking spray or a small amount of oil.
6. Place the shrimp toast triangles in Zone 1's cooking basket in a single layer.
7. Select Zone 1, choose the AIR FRY function, and set the temperature to 200°C. Set the cooking time to 10 minutes. Press the START/STOP.
8. Halfway through the cooking time, pause the air fryer and flip the shrimp toast triangles to ensure even browning. Then, continue cooking until they are crispy and golden brown.
9. Once the cooking time is complete, carefully remove the basket from the air fryer.
10. Garnish the Veggie Shrimp Toast with sesame seeds. Serve the **Veggie Shrimp Toast** as an appetizer or snack.

GARLIC-PARMESAN CROUTONS | SERVES 4

Prep time: 10 min | Cook time: 10 min

- 4 slices of bread, preferably a crusty variety like baguette or ciabatta
- 2 tablespoons olive oil
- 2 cloves garlic, minced
- 2 tablespoons grated Parmesan cheese
- 1/2 teaspoon dried Italian herbs
- Salt and pepper to taste.

DIRECTIONS:

1. Preheat the Ninja Dual Zone Air Fryer to 180°C in Zone 1 for a few minutes.
2. Cut the bread slices into bite-sized cubes or desired crouton shapes.
3. In a mixing bowl, combine the olive oil, minced garlic, grated Parmesan cheese, dried Italian herbs, salt, and pepper. Mix well to create a flavorful seasoning mixture.
4. Add the bread cubes to the seasoning mixture and toss until they are well coated.
5. Lightly grease the cooking basket in Zone 1 of the Ninja Dual Zone Air Fryer with cooking spray or a small amount of oil.
6. Place the seasoned bread cubes in Zone 1's cooking basket in a single layer.
7. Select Zone 1, choose the AIR FRY function, and set the temperature to 180°C. Set the cooking time to 10 minutes. Press the START/STOP button to begin cooking.
8. Halfway through the cooking time, pause the air fryer and shake the basket to ensure even cooking. Then, continue cooking until the croutons are crispy and golden brown.
9. Once the cooking time is complete, carefully remove the basket from the air fryer.
10. Allow the croutons to cool slightly before serving. They will continue to crisp up as they cool.
11. Serve the **Garlic-Parmesan Croutons** on salads, soups, or enjoy them as a crunchy snack.

LEMONY PEAR CHIPS | SERVES 4

Prep time: 10 min |Cook time: 120 min

- 2 large pears
- Juice of 1 lemon
- Zest of 1 lemon
- 2 tablespoons honey
- 1/2 teaspoon ground cinnamon.

DIRECTIONS:

1. Preheat the Ninja Dual Zone Air Fryer to 80°C in both zone for a few minutes.
2. Cut the pears into thin slices, about 1/8 inch thick. Remove any seeds or stems.
3. In a bowl, combine the lemon juice, lemon zest, honey, and ground cinnamon. Stir well to make a lemony marinade.
4. Place the pear slices in the marinade and gently toss them until they are evenly coated. Let them marinate for about 5 minutes.
5. Lightly grease the cooking basket in two zone of the Ninja Dual Zone Air Fryer with cooking spray or a small amount of oil.
6. Arrange the marinated pear slices in two zone cooking basket in a single layer, ensuring they do not overlap.
7. Select Zone 1, choose the DEHYDRATE function, and set the temperature to 80°C. Set the cooking time to 2 hours. Select MATCH. Press the START/STOP button to begin dehydrating.
8. After the first hour of cooking, pause the air fryer and flip the pear slices to ensure even dehydration. Then, continue dehydrating for the remaining hour.
9. Once the cooking time is complete, carefully remove the basket from the air fryer and let the pear chips cool completely. They will continue to crisp up as they cool.
10. Serve the **Lemony Pear Chips** as a healthy and flavorful snack.

SEA SALT POTATO CRISPS | SERVES 4

Prep time: 10 min |Cook time: 20 min

- 4 large potatoes (about 800g), preferably Maris Piper or King Edward
- 2 tablespoons olive oil
- Sea salt, to taste.

DIRECTIONS:

1. Preheat the Ninja Dual Zone Air Fryer to 200°C in two zone for a few minutes.
2. Wash and peel the potatoes. Slice them thinly, about 1/8 inch thick, using a sharp knife or a mandoline slicer.
3. Place the sliced potatoes in a large bowl of cold water and let them soak for 10 minutes. This helps remove excess starch and ensures crispy chips.
4. Drain the potatoes and pat them dry with a clean kitchen towel or paper towels.
5. In a separate bowl, toss the dried potato slices with olive oil until they are well coated.
6. Lightly grease the cooking basket in two zone of the Ninja Dual Zone Air Fryer with cooking spray or a small amount of oil.
7. Place the potato slices in both zone cooking basket in a single layer, ensuring they do not overlap.
8. Select Zone 1, choose the AIR FRY function, and set the temperature to 200°C. Set the cooking time to 15-20 minutes, depending on the desired level of crispiness. Select MATCH. Check the chips periodically and adjust the cooking time if needed.
9. Halfway through the cooking time, pause the air fryer and shake the basket to ensure even cooking. Then, continue cooking until the potato crisps are golden brown and crispy.
10. Once the cooking time is complete, carefully remove the basket from the air fryer. Sprinkle the hot potato crisps with sea salt, to taste.
11. Allow the potato crisps to cool slightly before serving. They will continue to crisp up as they cool.
12. Serve the **Sea Salt Potato Crisps** as a delicious snack or as a side dish to your favorite main course.

Chapter 9: Vegetables and Sides

CRISPY LEMON ARTICHOKE HEARTS | SERVES 2

- 1 can of artichoke hearts in water (400g), drained and rinsed
- 2 tablespoons plain flour
- 1/4 teaspoon garlic powder
- 1/4 teaspoon lemon zest
- 1/4 teaspoon dried thyme
- 1/4 teaspoon salt
- 1/8 teaspoon black pepper
- 1 egg, beaten
- 60g breadcrumbs
- Cooking spray or oil, for greasing.

Prep time: 10 min | Cook time: 15 min

DIRECTIONS

1. Pat dry the drained and rinsed artichoke hearts using a clean kitchen towel or paper towels.
2. In a shallow dish, combine the flour, garlic powder, lemon zest, dried thyme, salt, and black pepper. Mix well.
3. Dip each artichoke heart into the beaten egg, allowing any excess to drip off.
4. Coat the dipped artichoke hearts with the flour mixture, ensuring they are evenly coated.
5. In another shallow dish, place the breadcrumbs.
6. Roll the coated artichoke hearts in the breadcrumbs, pressing gently to adhere the breadcrumbs to the surface.
7. Lightly grease the cooking basket in Zone 1 of the Ninja Dual Zone Air Fryer with cooking spray or a small amount of oil.
8. Place the breaded artichoke hearts in Zone 1's cooking basket in a single layer, ensuring they do not overlap.
9. Select Zone 1, choose the AIR FRY, temperature to 200°C, cooking time to 12-15 minutes.
10. Halfway through the cooking time, pause the air fryer and shake the basket to ensure even browning. Then, continue cooking until the artichoke hearts are golden brown and crispy.
11. Once the cooking time is complete, carefully remove the basket from the air fryer and let the crispy lemon artichoke hearts cool for a few minutes.
12. Serve the **Crispy Lemon Artichoke Hearts** as a delicious appetizer or side dish. They can be enjoyed as is or with a dipping sauce of your choice.

SCALLOPED POTATOES
| SERVES 4

- 4 medium-sized potatoes (about 800g), peeled and thinly sliced
- 1 small onion, thinly sliced
- 2 cloves garlic, minced
- 500ml milk
- 250ml heavy cream
- 100g grated cheddar cheese
- 2 tablespoons butter
- 2 tablespoons all-purpose flour
- 1 teaspoon dried thyme
- Salt and pepper to taste.

Prep time: 15 min | Cook time: 30 min

DIRECTIONS

1. In a saucepan, melt the butter over medium heat. Add the minced garlic and sliced onion, and sauté until the onion becomes translucent.
2. Add the flour to the saucepan and cook for about 1-2 minutes, stirring continuously
3. Slowly pour in the milk and heavy cream while stirring to avoid lumps. Bring the mixture to a gentle simmer and cook for 2-3 minutes until it thickens slightly.
4. Stir in the grated cheddar cheese until melted and well combined. Season with dried thyme, salt, and pepper to taste.
5. Lightly grease a baking dish that fits in Zone 1 of Air Fryer.
6. Layer half of the sliced potatoes in the greased baking dish. Pour half of the cheese sauce over the potatoes, spreading it evenly.
7. Repeat with another layer of the remaining potatoes and pour the remaining cheese sauce on top.
8. Cover the baking dish with foil and place it in Zone 1.
9. Select Zone 1, choose the BAKE function, temperature to 180°C, cooking time to 30 minutes. Press the START/STOP.
10. After 20 minutes of cooking, remove the foil from the baking dish to allow the top to brown.
11. Continue baking for the remaining 10 minutes or until the potatoes are tender and the top is golden and crispy.
12. Once the cooking time is complete, carefully remove the baking dish from the air fryer using oven mitts or tongs.
13. Let the **Scalloped Potatoes** cool for a few minutes before serving.

GARLIC HERB RADISHES | SERVES 4

Prep time: 10 min | Cook time: 12 min

- 1 bunch of radishes (about 400g), washed and trimmed
- 2 tablespoons olive oil
- 2 cloves garlic, minced
- 1 teaspoon dried herbs (such as thyme, rosemary, or parsley)
- Salt and pepper to taste.

DIRECTIONS:

1. Cut the radishes into halves or quarters, depending on their size. Ensure they are relatively uniform in size for even cooking
2. In a bowl, combine the olive oil, minced garlic, dried herbs, salt, and pepper. Mix well to make the garlic herb seasoning.
3. Toss the radishes in the garlic herb seasoning until they are evenly coated.
4. Lightly grease the cooking basket in Zone 1 of the Ninja Dual Zone Air Fryer with cooking spray or a small amount of oil.
5. Place the seasoned radishes in Zone 1's cooking basket in a single layer, ensuring they are not overcrowded. (if overcrowded, put the rest to zone 2 and cook on both zones)
6. Select Zone 1, choose the AIR FRY, and set the temperature to 200°C. Set the time to 12 minutes. Press the START/STOP.
7. Halfway through the cooking time, pause the air fryer and shake the basket to ensure even cooking. Then, continue cooking until the radishes are tender and golden brown.
8. Once the cooking time is complete, carefully remove the basket from the air fryer and let the Garlic Herb Radishes cool for a few minutes.
9. Serve the **Garlic Herb Radishes** as a flavorful side dish or incorporate them into salads and other dishes.

CRISPY GARLIC SLICED AUBERGINE | SERVES 4

Prep time: 15 min | Cook time: 15 min

- 2 medium-sized aubergines (eggplants)
- 4 cloves garlic, minced
- 2 tablespoons olive oil
- 2 tablespoons breadcrumbs
- 1 tablespoon grated Parmesan cheese
- 1 teaspoon dried oregano
- Salt and pepper to taste.

DIRECTIONS:

1. Preheat the Air Fryer to 200°C in Zone 1 for a few minutes.
2. Wash the aubergines and cut them into 1/4-inch thick slices.
3. In a bowl, combine the minced garlic, olive oil, breadcrumbs, grated Parmesan cheese, dried oregano, salt, and pepper. Mix well to form a paste.
4. Brush both sides of the aubergine slices with the garlic paste mixture, ensuring they are well coated.
5. Lightly grease the air fryer basket in Zone 1 of the Ninja Dual Zone Air Fryer.
6. Place the coated aubergine slices in a single layer in the greased air fryer basket.
7. Select Zone 1, choose the AIR FRY function, temperature to 200°C, cooking time to 15 minutes.Press the START/STOP.
8. Halfway through the cooking time, flip the aubergine slices to ensure even browning.
9. After the cooking time is complete, carefully remove the crispy garlic sliced aubergine from the air fryer using tongs or a spatula.
10. Serve the **Crispy Garlic Sliced Aubergine** as a delicious side dish or as part of a meal. They are perfect for dipping in sauces or as a topping for salads.

POTATO WITH CREAMY CHEESE | SERVES 2

Prep time: 10 min | Cook time: 30 min

- 2 large potatoes, washed and thinly sliced
- 100g grated cheddar cheese
- 60ml sour cream
- 30g butter, melted
- 2 tablespoons chopped fresh chives
- Salt and pepper to taste.

DIRECTIONS:

1. In a bowl, combine the grated cheddar cheese, sour cream, melted butter, chopped fresh chives, salt, and pepper. Mix well to create a creamy cheese mixture.
2. Place the thinly sliced potatoes in a separate bowl and season them with salt and pepper.
3. Take one potato slice and spread a layer of the creamy cheese mixture on top. Place another potato slice on top and repeat the process until you have a stack of potato slices with the cheese mixture in between.
4. Repeat the process for the remaining potato slices and cheese mixture, creating multiple potato stacks.
5. Lightly grease the air fryer basket in Zone 1 of Air Fryer.
6. Place the potato stacks in a single layer in the greased air fryer basket.
7. Select Zone 1, choose the AIR FRY function, and set the temperature to 180°C, cooking time to 30 minutes. Press the START/STOP.
8. After the cooking time is complete, carefully remove the Potato with Creamy Cheese stacks from the air fryer using tongs or a spatula.
9. Serve the **Potato with Creamy Cheese** as a delightful side dish or as a main course. The potatoes will be crispy on the outside and tender on the inside, complemented by the creamy and cheesy filling.

BALSAMIC BRUSSELS SPROUTS | SERVES 4

Prep time: 10 min | Cook time: 15 min

- 500g Brussels sprouts, trimmed and halved
- 2 tablespoons olive oil
- 2 tablespoons balsamic vinegar
- 1 tablespoon honey
- 2 cloves garlic, minced
- Salt and pepper to taste.

DIRECTIONS:

1. Preheat the Ninja Dual Zone Air Fryer to 200°C in Zone 1 for a few minutes.
2. In a bowl, whisk together the olive oil, balsamic vinegar, honey, minced garlic, salt, and pepper to create a marinade.
3. Place the Brussels sprouts in a separate bowl and pour the marinade over them. Toss well to ensure the Brussels sprouts are evenly coated.
4. Lightly grease the air fryer basket in Zone 1.
5. Place the Brussels sprouts in a single layer in the greased air fryer basket. (if overcrowded, put the rest to zone 2 and cook on both zones)
6. Select Zone 1, choose the AIR FRY, set the temperature to 200°C, cooking time to 15 minutes. Press the START/STOP.
7. Halfway through the cooking time, gently shake the air fryer basket to ensure even cooking.
8. After the cooking time is complete, carefully remove the Balsamic Brussels Sprouts from the air fryer using tongs or a spatula.
9. Serve the **Balsamic Brussels Sprouts** as a delicious side dish. They will have a crispy exterior and a tender interior with a tangy and slightly sweet flavor from the balsamic marinade.

GOLD ARTICHOKE HEARTS | SERVES 4

Prep time: 10 min | Cook time: 15 min

- 2 cans of artichoke hearts (400g total), drained and rinsed
- 2 tablespoons olive oil
- 1 teaspoon garlic powder
- 1 teaspoon dried thyme
- 1/2 teaspoon salt
- 1/4 teaspoon black pepper
- Lemon wedges, for serving.

DIRECTIONS:

1. Preheat the Ninja Dual Zone Air Fryer to 200°C in Zone 1 for a few minutes.
2. In a bowl, combine the olive oil, garlic powder, dried thyme, salt, and black pepper.
3. Add the drained and rinsed artichoke hearts to the bowl and toss to coat them evenly with the seasoned oil mixture.
4. Lightly grease the air fryer basket in Zone 1. Place the seasoned artichoke hearts in the greased air fryer basket.
5. Select Zone 1, choose the AIR FRY function, set the temperature to 200°C, cooking time to 15 minutes. Press the START/STOP.
6. Halfway through the cooking time, gently shake the air fryer basket to ensure even cooking.
7. After the cooking time is complete, carefully remove the Gold Artichoke Hearts from the air fryer using tongs or a spatula.
8. Serve the crispy **Gold Artichoke Hearts** as a delightful appetizer or side dish. Squeeze fresh lemon juice over them for added flavor, if desired.

FRIED BRUSSELS SPROUTS | SERVES 4

Prep time: 10 min | Cook time: 15 min

- 500g Brussels sprouts, trimmed and halved
- 2 tablespoons olive oil
- 1 teaspoon garlic powder
- 1/2 teaspoon paprika
- 1/2 teaspoon salt
- 1/4 teaspoon black pepper
- Lemon wedges, for serving.

DIRECTIONS:

1. Preheat the Ninja Dual Zone Air Fryer to 200°C in Zone 1 for a few minutes.
2. In a large bowl, toss the Brussels sprouts with olive oil, garlic powder, paprika, salt, and black pepper until well coated.
3. Lightly grease the air fryer basket in Zone 1 of the Ninja Dual Zone Air Fryer.
4. Place the seasoned Brussels sprouts in the greased air fryer basket. (if overcrowded, put the rest to zone 2 and cook on both zones)
5. Select Zone 1, choose the AIR FRY function, set the temperature to 200°C, cooking time to 15 minutes. Press the START/STOP.
6. Halfway through the cooking time, gently shake the air fryer basket to ensure even cooking.
7. After the cooking time is complete, carefully remove the Fried Brussels Sprouts from the air fryer using tongs or a spatula.
8. Serve the crispy **Fried Brussels Sprouts** as a delicious side dish. Squeeze fresh lemon juice over them for added brightness, if desired.

DINNER ROLLS | SERVES 6

- 450g strong white bread flour
- 1 teaspoon salt
- 2 tablespoons granulated sugar
- 7g sachet fast-action dried yeast
- 250ml warm milk
- 50g unsalted butter, melted
- Olive oil, for greasing
- Egg wash (1 beaten egg mixed with 1 tablespoon milk), for brushing.

Prep time: 150 min | Cook time: 10 min

DIRECTIONS

1. In a large mixing bowl, combine the bread flour, salt, and sugar. Make a well in the center.
2. In a separate bowl, mix the dried yeast with warm milk and let it sit for a few minutes until it becomes frothy.
3. Pour the yeast mixture into the well of the dry ingredients. Add the melted butter.
4. Stir the mixture with a wooden spoon until it starts to come together, then use your hands to knead the dough in the bowl until it forms a smooth and elastic dough. You can also use a stand mixer with a dough hook attachment for this step.
5. Lightly flour a clean surface and turn out the dough onto it. Knead the dough for about 10 minutes until it becomes soft and elastic.
6. Grease a clean bowl with olive oil and place the dough in it. Cover the bowl with a clean kitchen towel or plastic wrap. Let the dough rise in a warm place for about 1 hour or until it has doubled in size.
7. After the dough has risen, gently punch it down to release any air bubbles. Transfer the dough onto a lightly floured surface.
8. Divide the dough into 6 equal portions. Shape each portion into a smooth ball by tucking the edges underneath.
9. Grease the air fryer basket in Zone 1 of the Ninja Dual Zone Air Fryer with olive oil. Place the shaped dough balls in a single layer in the greased basket, leaving space between them for expansion. Brush the tops of the dough balls with the egg wash.
10. Select Zone 1, choose the BAKE function, and set the temperature to 180°C. Set the cooking time to 10 minutes. Press the START/STOP button to begin baking.
11. Once the cooking time is complete, remove the Dinner Rolls from the air fryer and let them cool on a wire rack.
12. Serve the warm and freshly baked **Dinner Rolls** as a delightful addition to your meal.

DIJON ROAST CABBAGE | SERVES 4

Prep time: 10 min | Cook time: 20 min

- 1 small head of cabbage
- 2 tablespoons Dijon mustard
- 2 tablespoons olive oil
- 1 tablespoon honey
- 1 teaspoon garlic powder
- Salt and pepper to taste.

DIRECTIONS:

1. Preheat Zone 1 of the Ninja Dual Zone Air Fryer to 200°C.
2. Cut the cabbage into wedges, leaving the core intact to hold the wedges together.
3. In a small bowl, whisk together the Dijon mustard, olive oil, honey, garlic powder, salt, and pepper until well combined.
4. Brush the Dijon mustard mixture over the cabbage wedges, making sure to coat all sides.
5. Place the cabbage wedges in Zone 1 of the Ninja Dual Zone Air Fryer in a single layer.
6. Select Zone 1, choose the ROAST function, and set the temperature to 200°C. Set the cooking time to 20 minutes. Press the START/STOP button to begin roasting.
7. After 10 minutes of cooking, open Zone 1 and flip the cabbage wedges using tongs for even browning.
8. Close Zone 1 and continue roasting for the remaining 10 minutes or until the cabbage is tender and lightly charred.
9. Once done, remove the **Dijon Roast Cabbage** from the air fryer and serve hot as a delicious side dish.

CRISPY CHICKPEAS | SERVES 4

Prep time: 5 min | Cook time: 15 min

- 2 cans (400g each) chickpeas, drained and rinsed
- 2 tablespoons olive oil
- 1 teaspoon paprika
- 1/2 teaspoon cumin
- 1/2 teaspoon garlic powder
- 1/2 teaspoon onion powder
- 1/4 teaspoon cayenne pepper (adjust to taste)
- Salt to taste.

DIRECTIONS:

1. Preheat Zone 1 of the Ninja Dual Zone Air Fryer to 200°C.
2. In a bowl, toss the chickpeas with olive oil, paprika, cumin, garlic powder, onion powder, cayenne pepper, and salt until well coated.
3. Place the seasoned chickpeas in Zone 1 of the Ninja Dual Zone Air Fryer in a single layer.
4. Select Zone 1, choose the AIR FRY function, and set the temperature to 200°C. Set the cooking time to 15 minutes. Press the START/STOP.
5. After 7-8 minutes of cooking, open Zone 1 and shake the basket to ensure even cooking.
6. Close Zone 1 and continue air frying for the remaining 7-8 minutes or until the chickpeas are crispy and golden brown.
7. Once done, remove the crispy chickpeas from the air fryer and let them cool slightly before serving.
8. Serve the **crispy chickpeas** as a snack or use them as a topping for salads, soups, or roasted vegetables.

FRIED COURGETTE SALAD | SERVES 4

Prep time: 10 min | Cook time: 10 min

- 2 medium courgettes (zucchini), sliced into rounds
- 2 tablespoons plain flour
- 1/4 teaspoon salt
- 1/4 teaspoon black pepper
- 2 eggs, beaten
- 120g breadcrumbs
- 2 tablespoons grated Parmesan cheese
- 2 tablespoons olive oil
- Mixed salad greens
- Cherry tomatoes, halved
- Lemon wedges, for serving.

DIRECTIONS:

1. In a shallow bowl, combine the flour, salt, and black pepper. Place the beaten eggs in another bowl, and in a separate bowl, combine the breadcrumbs and grated Parmesan cheese.
2. Dip the courgette slices into the flour mixture, shaking off any excess. Then dip them into the beaten eggs, allowing any excess to drip off. Finally, coat the courgette slices in the breadcrumb mixture, pressing gently to adhere.
3. Place the coated courgette slices in Zone 1 of the Ninja Dual Zone Air Fryer in a single layer.
4. Select Zone 1, choose the AIR FRY function, and set the temperature to 200°C, cooking time to 10 minutes. Press the START/STOP.
5. After 5 minutes of cooking, open Zone 1 and flip the courgette slices to ensure even browning. Continue air frying for the remaining 5 minutes or until the courgettes are crispy and golden brown.
6. While the courgettes are frying, prepare the salad by combining mixed salad greens and cherry tomatoes in a serving bowl.
7. Once the courgettes are cooked, remove them from the air fryer and place them on a paper towel to absorb any excess oil.
8. Arrange the crispy courgette slices on top of the salad.
9. Serve the **fried courgette salad** with lemon wedges on the side for squeezing over the top.

RICOTTA POTATOES | SERVES 4

Prep time: 10 min | Cook time: 25 min

- 4 medium-sized potatoes, washed and scrubbed
- 120g ricotta cheese
- 2 tablespoons grated Parmesan cheese
- 2 tablespoons chopped fresh parsley
- 1 clove garlic, minced
- 1/2 teaspoon salt
- 1/4 teaspoon black pepper
- 2 tablespoons olive oil.

DIRECTIONS:

1. Pierce the potatoes all over with a fork. Place them in Zone 1, choose the AIR FRY, temperature to 200°C and cook for 20 minutes or until the potatoes are tender.
2. Once the potatoes are cooked, remove them from the air fryer and let them cool slightly.
3. Cut each potato in half lengthwise. Using a spoon, scoop out the flesh of each potato, leaving a thin layer of potato intact along the skin.
4. In a bowl, combine the potato flesh, ricotta cheese, grated Parmesan cheese, chopped parsley, minced garlic, salt, and black pepper. Mix well until all ingredients are thoroughly combined.
5. Spoon the ricotta mixture back into the potato skins, filling them generously.
6. Place the stuffed potato halves in Zone 1. Select Zone 1, choose the AIR FRY, temperature to 200°C, cooking time to 5 minutes. Press the START/STOP.
7. After 2 minutes of cooking, open Zone 1 and drizzle the olive oil over the stuffed potato halves. Continue air frying for the remaining 3 minutes or until the tops are golden brown.
8. Once cooked, remove the **ricotta potatoes** from the air fryer and serve them hot.

BUTTER AND GARLIC FRIED CABBAGE | SERVES 2

Prep time: 10 min | Cook time: 12 min

- 1/2 small cabbage head, thinly sliced
- 2 tablespoons butter
- 2 cloves garlic, minced
- 1/2 teaspoon salt
- 1/4 teaspoon black pepper
- 1/4 teaspoon paprika (optional)

DIRECTIONS:

1. Preheat Zone 1 of the Ninja Dual Zone Air Fryer to 180°C. (use AIR FRY function)
2. In a large bowl, toss the sliced cabbage with salt, black pepper, and paprika (if using).
3. Place the butter in Zone 1 of the Ninja Dual Zone Air Fryer and let it melt. (about 1 minutes)
4. Add the minced garlic to the melted butter and sauté for 2 minute, until fragrant.
5. Add the seasoned cabbage to the air fryer basket in Zone 1. Close Zone 1.
6. Select Zone 1, choose the AIR FRY function, and set the temperature to 180°C. Set the cooking time to 12 minutes. Press the START/STOP button to begin air frying.
7. Every 4 minutes, open Zone 1 and give the cabbage a stir to ensure even cooking.
8. After 12 minutes of cooking, check the cabbage for desired tenderness. If needed, continue cooking for an additional 2-3 minutes.
9. Once cooked to your liking, remove the **butter and garlic fried cabbage** from the air fryer and serve it hot.

LEBANESE BABA GHANOUSH | SERVES 4

Prep time: 10 min | Cook time: 30 min

- 2 large aubergines (eggplants)
- 2 garlic cloves, minced
- 3 tablespoons tahini
- 2 tablespoons freshly squeezed lemon juice
- 2 tablespoons extra-virgin olive oil
- 1/2 teaspoon ground cumin
- Salt, to taste
- Fresh parsley, for garnish
- Extra olive oil, for drizzling.

DIRECTIONS:

1. Using a fork, prick the aubergines all over. This will allow steam to escape during cooking and prevent them from bursting.
2. Place the aubergines in the zone 1 basket, choose ROAST function, temperature to 200°C and cooking time to 25 minutes or until the skin is charred and the flesh is soft and cooked through.
3. Flip them halfway through cooking for even browning.
4. Remove the cooked aubergines from air fryer and let them cool slightly. Once cool enough to handle, cut the aubergines in half lengthwise and scoop out the flesh using a spoon. Discard the charred skin.
5. Place the aubergine flesh in a colander or sieve to drain excess liquid for about 10 minutes.
6. In a food processor, combine the drained aubergine, minced garlic, tahini, lemon juice, olive oil, ground cumin, and salt. Pulse until well blended and creamy. Taste and adjust the seasonings if needed.
7. Transfer the Baba Ghanoush to a serving dish. Garnish with fresh parsley and drizzle with some extra olive oil.
8. Serve the **Lebanese Baba Ghanoush** with pita bread, crackers, or fresh vegetables for dipping.

MUSHROOMS WITH GOAT CHEESE | SERVES 4

Prep time: 10 min | Cook time: 15 min

- 8 large mushrooms, cleaned and stems removed
- 100g goat cheese, crumbled
- 2 tablespoons fresh parsley, chopped
- 2 tablespoons breadcrumbs
- 2 tablespoons grated Parmesan cheese
- 2 cloves of garlic, minced
- 2 tablespoons olive oil
- Salt and pepper, to taste.

DIRECTIONS:

1. In a bowl, combine the goat cheese, fresh parsley, breadcrumbs, grated Parmesan cheese, minced garlic, olive oil, salt, and pepper. Mix well until all the ingredients are evenly incorporated.
2. Stuff each mushroom cap with the prepared goat cheese mixture, filling it generously.
3. Place the stuffed mushrooms in Zone 1 of the air fryer basket.
4. Select Zone 1, choose the AIR FRY function, and set the temperature to 180°C. Set the cooking time to 12-15 minutes (until the mushrooms are tender and the cheese is melted and slightly golden). Press the START/STOP button to begin air frying.
5. Once cooked, remove the mushrooms from the air fryer and let them cool slightly.
6. Serve the **mushrooms with goat cheese** as a delicious appetizer or side dish.

GREEN TOMATO SALAD | SERVES 4

Prep time: 15 min | Cook time: 10 min

- 4 green tomatoes
- 1 small red onion
- 1/2 cucumber
- 25g fresh parsley, chopped
- 25g fresh mint leaves, chopped
- Juice of 1 lemon
- 2 tablespoons extra virgin olive oil
- Salt and pepper to taste.

DIRECTIONS:

1. Slice the green tomatoes into thin rounds. Finely chop the red onion. Cut the cucumber in half lengthwise, remove the seeds, and slice it into thin half-moons.
2. In a mixing bowl, combine the sliced green tomatoes, red onion, cucumber, chopped parsley, and chopped mint leaves.
3. In a separate small bowl, whisk together the lemon juice, extra virgin olive oil, salt, and pepper to make the dressing.
4. Pour the dressing over the salad mixture and toss well to combine, ensuring all the ingredients are coated evenly.
5. Place the salad plate in Zone 1. Set Zone 1 to the AIR FRY function, and adjust the temperature to 200°C. Cook for 10 minutes or until the tomatoes have softened slightly.
6. Once cooked, remove the plate from the air fryer.
7. Serve the **Green Tomato Salad** immediately as a refreshing side dish or appetizer.

GLAZED SWEET POTATO BITES | SERVES 4

Prep time: 15 min | Cook time: 20 min

- 2 medium-sized sweet potatoes
- 2 tablespoons olive oil
- 2 tablespoons maple syrup
- 1 teaspoon ground cinnamon
- 1/2 teaspoon ground nutmeg
- 1/2 teaspoon salt
- 1/4 teaspoon black pepper
- Fresh parsley or coriander leaves for garnish (optional)

DIRECTIONS:

1. Peel the sweet potatoes and cut them into bite-sized cubes.
2. In a large bowl, combine the olive oil, maple syrup, ground cinnamon, ground nutmeg, salt, and black pepper. Mix well.
3. Add the sweet potato cubes to the bowl and toss them in the glaze mixture until they are evenly coated.
4. Preheat Zone 1 to 200°C.
5. Place the sweet potato cubes in Zone 1. Make sure they are arranged in a single layer for even cooking.
6. Select Zone 1, choose the AIR FRY function, set the temperature to 200°C. Time to 20 minutes. Flipping the sweet potato cubes halfway through the cooking time for even browning.
7. Once the sweet potato bites are crispy and caramelized, remove them from the air fryer and let them cool slightly.
8. Transfer the glazed sweet potato bites to a serving dish and garnish with fresh parsley or coriander leaves, if desired.
9. Serve the **Glazed Sweet Potato Bites** as a delicious side dish or appetizer.

CHEESE-WALNUT STUFFED MUSHROOMS | SERVES 4

Prep time: 15 min | Cook time: 12 min

- 8 large button mushrooms
- 50g grated cheddar cheese
- 25g breadcrumbs
- 25g chopped walnuts
- 1 tablespoon chopped fresh parsley
- 1 clove garlic, minced
- 1 tablespoon olive oil
- Salt and pepper to taste.

DIRECTIONS:

1. Remove the stems from the mushrooms and set them aside.
2. In a mixing bowl, combine the grated cheddar cheese, breadcrumbs, chopped walnuts, chopped parsley, minced garlic, olive oil, salt, and pepper. Mix well to form a stuffing mixture.
3. Fill each mushroom cap with a generous amount of the cheese-walnut stuffing mixture, pressing it gently to ensure it stays in place.
4. Finely chop the reserved mushroom stems and distribute them evenly over the stuffed mushrooms.
5. Place the stuffed mushrooms in Zone 1 of the Ninja Dual Zone air fryer. Make sure they are arranged in a single layer.
6. Select Zone 1, choose the AIR FRY function, set the temperature to 180°C. Time to 12 minutes, until the mushrooms are tender and the cheese is melted and lightly golden.
7. Once cooked, carefully remove the stuffed mushrooms from the air fryer and let them cool for a few minutes before serving.
8. Serve the **Cheese-Walnut Stuffed Mushrooms** as a delicious appetizer or side dish.

LUSH VEGETABLE SALAD | SERVES 4

Prep time: 15 min | Cook time: 8 min

- 200g cherry tomatoes, halved
- 1 large cucumber, diced
- 1 red bell pepper, diced
- 1 yellow bell pepper, diced
- 1 small red onion, thinly sliced
- 100g feta cheese, crumbled
- 50g pitted black olives
- 2 tablespoons extra virgin olive oil
- 1 tablespoon lemon juice
- 1 teaspoon dried oregano
- Salt and pepper to taste
- Fresh parsley, chopped (for garnish)

DIRECTIONS:

1. In a large mixing bowl, combine the cherry tomatoes, diced cucumber, diced red bell pepper, diced yellow bell pepper, and thinly sliced red onion.
2. In a small bowl, whisk together the extra virgin olive oil, lemon juice, dried oregano, salt, and pepper to make the dressing.
3. Pour the dressing over the vegetable mixture and toss gently to coat all the vegetables evenly.
4. Place the vegetable mixture in Zone 1 of the air fryer, spreading it out in a single layer.
5. Select Zone 1, choose the AIR FRY function, and set the temperature to 180°C. Set the cooking time to 8 minutes (until the vegetables are slightly softened and lightly charred). Press the START/STOP.
6. Once cooked, remove the vegetable mixture from the air fryer and let it cool for a few minutes.
7. Transfer the vegetable mixture to a serving dish and sprinkle crumbled feta cheese and black olives on top.
8. Garnish with fresh parsley and serve the **Lush Vegetable Salad** as a refreshing and nutritious side dish or light lunch.

CORN AND CORIANDER SALAD | SERVES 2

Prep time: 10 min | Cook time: 6 min

- 2 ears of corn, husked
- 1 small red onion, finely chopped
- 1 small red bell pepper, finely chopped
- 1 small green bell pepper, finely chopped
- 4 tablespoons fresh coriander (cilantro), chopped
- 2 tablespoons lime juice
- 2 tablespoons extra virgin olive oil
- Salt and pepper to taste.

DIRECTIONS:

1. Place the corn ears in Zone 1. Select Zone 1, choose the ROAST function, and set the temperature to 200°C, time to 8 minutes or until the corn kernels are tender and slightly charred.
2. Turn the corn ears halfway through cooking for even browning.
3. Once cooked, remove the corn ears from the air fryer and let them cool slightly.
4. Using a sharp knife, carefully cut the kernels off the cobs and transfer them to a large mixing bowl.
5. Add the chopped red onion, red bell pepper, green bell pepper, and fresh coriander to the bowl with the corn kernels.
6. In a separate small bowl, whisk together the lime juice, extra virgin olive oil, salt, and pepper to make the dressing.
7. Pour the dressing over the corn and vegetable mixture and toss gently to coat everything evenly.
8. Let the salad marinate for a few minutes to allow the flavors to meld together.
9. Serve the **Corn and Coriander Salad** as a refreshing side dish or light lunch option.

BUFFALO CAULIFLOWER WITH BLUE CHEESE | SERVES 6

- 1 large head of cauliflower, cut into florets
- 125g plain flour
- 1 teaspoon garlic powder
- 1 teaspoon onion powder
- 1/2 teaspoon paprika
- 1/2 teaspoon salt
- 1/4 teaspoon black pepper
- 240ml milk (or plant-based milk for a vegan version)
- 120ml hot sauce (such as Frank's RedHot)
- 60g crumbled blue cheese (or dairy-free blue cheese for a vegan version)
- 60g melted butter (or vegan butter for a vegan version)
- Fresh parsley, chopped (for garnish).

Prep time: 15 min | Cook time: 15 min

DIRECTIONS

1. In a large mixing bowl, combine the flour, garlic powder, onion powder, paprika, salt, and black pepper.
2. Dip each cauliflower floret into the milk, then roll it in the flour mixture until evenly coated. Shake off any excess flour.
3. Place the coated cauliflower florets in Zone 1 of the air fryer basket in a single layer. (if overcrowded, put the rest to zone 2 and cook on both zones).
4. Select Zone 1, choose the AIR FRY, and set the temperature to 200°C. Set the time to 15 minutes (or until the cauliflower is crispy and golden brown). Press the START/STOP.
5. Shake the basket halfway through cooking for even browning.
6. While the cauliflower is cooking, prepare the buffalo sauce. In a small saucepan, heat the hot sauce and melted butter over low heat until well combined.
7. Once the cauliflower is cooked, transfer it to a large mixing bowl. Pour the buffalo sauce over the cauliflower and toss to coat evenly.
8. Return the coated cauliflower to the air fryer basket in Zone 1. choose the AIR FRY, and set the temperature to 200°C, cook for an additional 5 minutes to allow the sauce to adhere and the flavors to meld.
9. Remove the buffalo cauliflower from the air fryer and sprinkle the crumbled blue cheese over the top.
10. Garnish with fresh parsley and serve hot as a delicious appetizer or side dish.
11. This **Buffalo Cauliflower with Blue Cheese** recipe offers a tasty twist on traditional buffalo wings, The crispy cauliflower florets are coated in a spicy buffalo sauce and topped with tangy blue cheese crumbles. Enjoy!

Chapter 10: Vegetarian Mains

PESTO SPINACH FLATBREAD | SERVES 4

Prep time: 15 min | Cook time: 10 min

- 250g pre-made pizza dough (store-bought or homemade)
- 120g pesto sauce
- 50g baby spinach leaves
- 75g cherry tomatoes, halved
- 50g sliced red onion
- 100g shredded mozzarella cheese
- 25g grated Parmesan cheese
- 1/4 teaspoon dried oregano
- Salt and pepper to taste
- Olive oil for brushing.

DIRECTIONS:

1. On a lightly floured surface, roll out the pizza dough into a rectangular shape, about 1/4 inch thick.
2. Carefully transfer the rolled-out dough to basket of Zone 1.
3. Spread the pesto sauce evenly over the surface of the dough, leaving a small border around the edges.
4. Layer the baby spinach leaves, cherry tomatoes, and red onion slices over the pesto sauce.
5. Sprinkle the shredded mozzarella cheese and grated Parmesan cheese on top of the vegetables. Season with dried oregano, salt, and pepper to taste.
6. Place the air fryer basket in Zone 1. Select Zone 1, choose the AIR FRY, set the temperature to 200°C, cooking time to 10 minutes (until it turns golden brown and the cheese has melted). Press the START/STOP.
7. Once cooked, carefully remove the flatbread from Zone 1 using tongs or a spatula.
8. Brush the edges of the flatbread with olive oil for added flavor and shine.
9. Allow the **Pesto Spinach Flatbread** to cool for a few minutes, then cut it into desired portions and serve.

STUFFED PORTOBELLOS | SERVES 4

Prep time: 15 min | Cook time: 15 min

- 4 large Portobello mushrooms
- 200g fresh spinach
- 150g feta cheese, crumbled
- 1 red bell pepper, diced
- 1 small red onion, diced
- 2 cloves garlic, minced
- 2 tablespoons olive oil
- 1 teaspoon dried thyme
- Salt and pepper to taste.

DIRECTIONS:

1. Clean the Portobello mushrooms and remove the stems. Set them aside.
2. In a pan, heat 1 tablespoon of olive oil over medium heat. Add the diced red bell pepper, red onion, and minced garlic. Sauté until softened and fragrant.
3. Add the fresh spinach to the pan and cook until wilted. Season with salt, pepper, and dried thyme. Remove from heat and set aside.
4. In a separate bowl, crumble the feta cheese.
5. Brush the Portobello mushroom caps with the remaining olive oil. Place them in Zone 1 of the air fryer basket.
6. Fill each mushroom cap with the sautéed spinach mixture and top with crumbled feta cheese.
7. Select Zone 1, choose the AIR FRY, set the temperature to 180°C, cooking time to 15 minutes (until the mushrooms are tender and the cheese is melted and slightly golden.). Press the START/STOP.
8. Once cooked, carefully remove the **Stuffed Portobellos** from Zone 1 using tongs or a spatula.
9. Allow the stuffed mushrooms to cool for a few minutes before serving.

QUICHE-STUFFED PEPPERS | SERVES 2

Prep time: 15 min | Cook time: 20 min

- 2 large bell peppers (red, yellow, or orange)
- 4 large eggs
- 100ml milk
- 75g shredded cheddar cheese
- 50g diced cooked ham
- 50g diced red onion
- 50g diced cherry tomatoes
- 1 tablespoon chopped fresh parsley
- Salt and pepper to taste.

DIRECTIONS:

1. Cut off the tops of the bell peppers and remove the seeds and membranes from the inside. Set aside.
2. In a bowl, whisk together the eggs and milk. Season with salt and pepper.
3. Add the shredded cheddar cheese, diced cooked ham, diced red onion, diced cherry tomatoes, and chopped fresh parsley to the egg mixture. Stir well to combine.
4. Place the bell peppers in basket of Zone 1.
5. Carefully pour the quiche mixture into each bell pepper, filling them about 3/4 full.
6. Place the air fryer basket in Zone 1 of the Ninja Dual Zone air fryer.
7. Select Zone 1, choose the AIR FRY function, and set the temperature to 180°C. Set the cooking time to 20 minutes (until the eggs are set and the tops are slightly golden). Press the START/STOP.
8. Once cooked, carefully remove the **Quiche-Stuffed Peppers** from Zone 1 using tongs or a spatula.
9. Allow them to cool for a few minutes before serving.

RUSSET POTATO GRATIN | SERVES 6

Prep time: 20 min | Cook time: 45 min

- 1 kg Russet potatoes, peeled and thinly sliced
- 300 ml double cream
- 200 ml whole milk
- 150g shredded cheddar cheese
- 2 cloves garlic, minced
- 1 tablespoon fresh thyme leaves
- Salt and pepper to taste
- Butter for greasing.

DIRECTIONS:

1. Grease a baking dish with butter. Set it aside.
2. In a saucepan, heat the double cream, whole milk, minced garlic, and fresh thyme leaves over medium heat until hot but not boiling. Season with salt and pepper to taste.
3. Layer half of the sliced potatoes in the greased baking dish.
4. Pour half of the hot cream mixture over the potatoes, ensuring they are evenly coated.
5. Sprinkle half of the shredded cheddar cheese on top.
6. Layer the remaining sliced potatoes on top, followed by the remaining hot cream mixture.
7. Sprinkle the remaining shredded cheddar cheese over the top.
8. Place the baking dish in Zone 1. Select Zone 1, choose the AIR FRY, set the temperature to 180°C, cooking time to 45 minutes (until the potatoes are tender and the top is golden and bubbly). Press the START/STOP.
9. Once cooked, carefully remove the potato gratin from Zone 1 using oven mitts or tongs.
10. Allow **Russet Potato Gratin** to cool for a few minutes before serving.

SUPER VEGETABLE BURGER | SERVES 8

- 400g canned chickpeas, drained and rinsed
- 200g canned black beans, drained and rinsed
- 200g cooked quinoa
- 100g grated carrots
- 100g grated zucchini
- 100g chopped mushrooms
- 50g diced red onion
- 2 cloves garlic, minced
- 50g breadcrumbs
- 2 tablespoons chopped fresh parsley
- 1 teaspoon ground cumin
- 1 teaspoon paprika
- Salt and pepper to taste
- Burger buns and toppings of your choice (lettuce, tomato, onion, etc.)

Prep time: 15 min | Cook time: 15 min

DIRECTIONS

1. Select Zone 1, choose the AIR FRY program, and preheat the air fryer to 200°C. Select MATCH to duplicate settings across both zones.
2. In a large bowl, mash the chickpeas and black beans with a fork or potato masher until chunky.
3. Add the cooked quinoa, grated carrots, grated zucchini, chopped mushrooms, diced red onion, minced garlic, breadcrumbs, chopped fresh parsley, ground cumin, paprika, salt, and pepper to the bowl. Mix well to combine all the ingredients.
4. Shape the mixture into 8 equal-sized patties, pressing them firmly to hold their shape.
5. Evenly dividing and place the vegetable patties in two zone of the air fryer basket.
6. Select Zone 1, choose the AIR FRY, and set the temperature to 200°C. Set the time to 15 minutes. Select MATCH. Press the START/STOP.
7. Flipping them halfway through, until they are golden brown and crispy.
8. Once cooked, carefully remove the vegetable burgers using a spatula.
9. Serve the **Super Vegetable Burgers** on burger buns with your choice of toppings, such as lettuce, tomato, and onion.

CHEESE STUFFED PEPPERS | SERVES 2

Prep time: 25 min | Cook time: 15 min

- 2 large bell peppers (red, yellow, or orange)
- 100g cream cheese
- 50g grated cheddar cheese
- 2 tablespoons grated Parmesan cheese
- 1 tablespoon chopped fresh basil
- 1 tablespoon chopped fresh parsley
- 1/2 teaspoon garlic powder
- Salt and pepper to taste.

DIRECTIONS:

1. Cut off the tops of the bell peppers and remove the seeds and membranes from the inside. Set aside.
2. In a bowl, combine the cream cheese, grated cheddar cheese, grated Parmesan cheese, chopped fresh basil, chopped fresh parsley, garlic powder, salt, and pepper. Mix well to create a creamy filling.
3. Stuff each bell pepper with the cheese filling, ensuring they are evenly filled.
4. Place the stuffed peppers in basket of Zone 1. Select Zone 1, choose the AIR FRY function, and set the temperature to 180°C. Set the cooking time to 15 minutes (until the peppers are tender and the cheese filling is melted and slightly golden). Press the START/STOP button to begin cooking.
5. Once cooked, carefully remove the cheese stuffed peppers from Zone 1 using tongs or a spatula.
6. Allow the **Cheese Stuffed Peppers** to cool for a few minutes before serving.

MEDITERRANEAN AIR FRIED VEGGIES | SERVES 4

Prep time: 15 min | Cook time: 12 min

- 2 medium zucchini, sliced into rounds
- 1 large red bell pepper, sliced into strips
- 1 large yellow bell pepper, sliced into strips
- 1 red onion, cut into wedges
- 200g cherry tomatoes
- 2 tablespoons olive oil
- 2 cloves garlic, minced
- 1 teaspoon dried oregano
- 1 teaspoon dried basil
- Salt and pepper to taste
- Fresh parsley, for garnish.

DIRECTIONS:

1. In a large bowl, combine the sliced zucchini, red and yellow bell peppers, red onion wedges, cherry tomatoes, olive oil, minced garlic, dried oregano, dried basil, salt, and pepper. Toss well to coat the vegetables evenly with the seasonings and oil.
2. Select Zone 1, choose the AIR FRY program, and preheat the air fryer to 200°C
3. Place the seasoned vegetables in basket of Zone 1.
4. Select Zone 1, choose the AIR FRY function, and set the temperature to 200°C. Set the cooking time to 12 minutes. Press the START/STOP button to begin cooking.
5. Shaking the basket or stirring the veggies halfway through to ensure even cooking.
6. Once cooked, carefully remove the **Mediterranean Air Fried Veggies** from Zone 1 using tongs or a spatula.
7. Garnish with fresh parsley and serve as a side dish or as a topping for salads, wraps, or sandwiches.

CHEESY CABBAGE WEDGES | SERVES 4

Prep time: 10 min | Cook time: 15 min

- 1 medium green cabbage
- 4 tablespoons melted butter
- 1 teaspoon garlic powder
- 1 teaspoon paprika
- Salt and pepper to taste
- 100g grated cheddar cheese
- Fresh parsley, for garnish.

DIRECTIONS:

1. Cut the cabbage into quarters, leaving the core intact to hold the wedges together.
2. In a small bowl, combine the melted butter, garlic powder, paprika, salt, and pepper. Mix well.
3. Brush the melted butter mixture onto all sides of the cabbage wedges, ensuring they are evenly coated.
4. Place the seasoned cabbage wedges in Zone 1 of the air fryer.
5. Select Zone 1, choose the AIR FRY function, and set the temperature to 200°C. Set the cooking time to 15 minutes (until they are tender and lightly charred on the edges). Press the START/STOP.
6. Once cooked, carefully remove the cabbage wedges from Zone 1 using tongs or a spatula.
7. Sprinkle the grated cheddar cheese over the cabbage wedges, allowing it to melt slightly from the residual heat.
8. Garnish with fresh parsley. Enjoy **Cheesy Cabbage Wedges**!

NOTE: *When place the seasoned cabbage wedges in Zone 1, if they are too crowded, put the rest in zone 2 and cook on both zones. Don't forget to Select MATCH to duplicate settings across both zones*

CAULIFLOWER RICE-STUFFED PEPPERS | SERVES 4

Prep time: 20 min | Cook time: 15 min

- 4 large bell peppers (red, yellow, or orange)
- 1 cauliflower head
- 1 tablespoon olive oil
- 1 small onion, diced
- 2 cloves garlic, minced
- 200g mushrooms, sliced
- 1 teaspoon dried oregano
- 1 teaspoon dried basil
- Salt and pepper to taste
- 100g grated cheddar cheese
- Fresh parsley, for garnish.

DIRECTIONS:

1. Cut off the tops of the bell peppers and remove the seeds and membranes from the inside. Set aside.
2. Cut the cauliflower into florets and place them in a food processor. Pulse until the cauliflower resembles rice-like grains.
3. In a large skillet, heat the olive oil over medium heat. Add the diced onion and minced garlic, and sauté until softened and fragrant. Add the sliced mushrooms to the skillet and cook until they are golden brown and tender.
4. Add the cauliflower rice, dried oregano, dried basil, salt, and pepper to the skillet. Cook for about 5 minutes, stirring occasionally, until the cauliflower rice is tender.
5. Spoon the cauliflower rice mixture into the bell peppers, dividing it evenly among them.
6. Place the stuffed peppers in Zone 1 of the air fryer.
7. Select Zone 1, choose the AIR FRY function, and set the temperature to 180°C, cooking time to 15 minutes (until the peppers are tender and slightly charred). Press the START/STOP.
8. Once cooked, carefully remove the stuffed peppers from Zone 1 using tongs or a spatula.
9. Sprinkle the grated cheddar cheese over the stuffed peppers, allowing it to melt slightly from the residual heat.
10. Enjoy **Cauliflower Rice-Stuffed Peppers**!

AUBERGINE AND COURGETTE BITES
| SERVES 8

- 1 large aubergine (eggplant), sliced into 1/4-inch (6mm) thick rounds
- 2 medium courgettes (zucchini), sliced into 1/4-inch (6mm) thick rounds
- 30 ml olive oil
- 3 teaspoons dried oregano
- 1/2 teaspoon garlic powder
- 1/2 teaspoon salt
- 1/4 teaspoon black pepper
- 25 g grated Parmesan cheese
- Fresh basil leaves, for garnish (optional)

Prep time: 15 min | Cook time: 15 min

DIRECTIONS

1. In a bowl, toss the aubergine and courgette slices with olive oil, dried oregano, garlic powder, salt, and black pepper until well coated.
2. Grease the air fryer basket in both zone with a small amount of oil or use a parchment liner to prevent sticking.
3. Evenly dividing the seasoned aubergine and courgette slices, and place them in a single layer in two zone of the air fryer.
4. Select Zone 1, choose the AIR FRY function, set temperature to 200°C, time to 15 minutes, select MATCH to duplicate settings across both zones and press the START/STOP button to begin air frying.
5. Check aubergine and courgette slices until they are tender and slightly golden brown, flipping them halfway through the cooking time.
6. Once cooked, carefully remove the air fryer baskets using oven mitts or tongs.
7. Sprinkle the grated Parmesan cheese evenly over the cooked aubergine and courgette slices while they are still hot.
8. Allow the bites to cool slightly before serving.
9. Garnish with fresh basil leaves, if desired.
10. Enjoy **Aubergine and Courgette Bites**!

Chapter 11: Desserts

PUMPKIN PUDDING WITH VANILLA WAFERS | SERVES 4

Prep time: 10 min | Cook time: 20 min

- 400g canned pumpkin puree
- 200ml double cream
- 100g light brown sugar
- 2 large eggs
- 1 teaspoon vanilla extract
- 1 teaspoon pumpkin pie spice
- A pinch of salt
- 16 vanilla wafers
- Whipped cream, for serving (optional)
- Ground cinnamon, for garnish (optional)

DIRECTIONS:

1. In a mixing bowl, combine the pumpkin puree, double cream, light brown sugar, eggs, vanilla extract, pumpkin pie spice, and salt. Whisk together until well combined and smooth.
2. Grease 4 individual ramekins or oven-safe dishes.
3. Place 4 vanilla wafers at the bottom of each greased ramekin.
4. Pour the pumpkin pudding mixture over the vanilla wafers, dividing it equally among the ramekins.
5. Place the filled ramekins in Zone 1. Select the BAKE function and set the temperature to 180°C. Set the cooking time to 20 minutes and press the START/STOP button to begin baking.
6. Once the cooking time is complete, carefully remove the ramekins from the air fryer using oven mitts or tongs.
7. Allow the **pumpkin pudding** to cool to room temperature, then refrigerate for at least 2 hours to chill and set.
8. Just before serving, garnish with a dollop of whipped cream and a sprinkle of ground cinnamon, if desired.

SHORTCUT SPICED APPLE BUTTER | MAKES 4 CUPS

Prep time: 20 min | Cook time: 180 min

- 1kg cooking apples (such as Bramley), peeled, cored, and chopped
- 150g light brown sugar
- 1 teaspoon ground cinnamon
- 1/2 teaspoon ground nutmeg
- 1/4 teaspoon ground cloves
- Juice of 1 lemon
- 1/2 teaspoon vanilla extract.

DIRECTIONS:

1. In a large mixing bowl, combine the chopped apples, light brown sugar, ground cinnamon, ground nutmeg, ground cloves, lemon juice, and vanilla extract. Stir well to coat the apples with the spices.
2. Place the apple mixture in Zone 1 of the air fryer. Select Zone 1, choose the AIR FRY function, and set the temperature to 160°C. Cook for 90 minutes, stirring occasionally, until the apples are soft and have reduced in volume.
3. Once the apples are cooked, carefully transfer them to a blender or food processor. Blend until smooth and creamy.
4. Return the blended apple mixture to the Ninja Dual Zone air fryer. Select the AIR FRY function in Zone 1 (temperature to 160°C) and cook for an additional 90 minutes, stirring occasionally, until the apple butter thickens to your desired consistency.
5. Once the apple butter has reached the desired consistency, carefully remove the air fryer basket from Zone 1 of the Ninja Dual Zone.
6. Allow the **apple butter** to cool completely before transferring it to clean, sterilized jars.
7. Store the apple butter in the refrigerator for up to 2 weeks or preserve it using proper canning techniques for longer shelf life.

GINGERBREAD | MAKES 1 LOAF

Prep time: 15 min | Cook time: 35 min

- 225g plain flour
- 1 teaspoon ground ginger
- 1 teaspoon ground cinnamon
- 1/2 teaspoon ground nutmeg
- 1/2 teaspoon baking soda
- 1/4 teaspoon salt
- 115g unsalted butter, softened
- 115g light brown sugar
- 2 large eggs
- 4 tablespoons golden syrup
- 120ml whole milk.

DIRECTIONS:

1. In a mixing bowl, whisk together the plain flour, ground ginger, ground cinnamon, ground nutmeg, baking soda, and salt until well combined.
2. In a separate large mixing bowl, cream together the softened butter and light brown sugar until light and fluffy.
3. Add the eggs to the butter mixture, one at a time, beating well after each addition. Stir in the golden syrup.
4. Gradually add the dry ingredient mixture to the wet mixture, alternating with the whole milk. Mix until just combined, being careful not to overmix.
5. Grease and line a loaf pan that fits in Zone 1 of the air fryer.
6. Pour the gingerbread batter into the prepared loaf pan.
7. Place the loaf pan in Zone 1. Select Zone 1, choose BAKE, and set the temperature to 200°C. Set the cooking time to 35 minutes (until a toothpick inserted into the center comes out clean). Press the START/STOP.
8. Once baked, carefully remove the loaf pan from the air fryer and allow the gingerbread to cool in the pan for a few minutes before transferring it to a wire rack to cool completely.
9. Once cooled, slice and serve the **gingerbread** as desired.

WHITE CHOCOLATE COOKIES | SERVES 10

Prep time: 15 min | Cook time: 12 min

- 115g unsalted butter, softened
- 100g light brown sugar
- 100g granulated sugar
- 1 large egg
- 1 teaspoon vanilla extract
- 225g plain flour
- 1/2 teaspoon baking soda
- 1/4 teaspoon salt
- 150g white chocolate chips.

DIRECTIONS:

1. In a large mixing bowl, cream together the softened butter, light brown sugar, and granulated sugar until light and fluffy.
2. Add the egg and vanilla extract to the butter mixture. Beat well until fully incorporated.
3. In a separate bowl, whisk together the plain flour, baking soda, and salt.
4. Gradually add the dry ingredient mixture to the wet mixture, mixing until just combined.
5. Fold in the white chocolate chips until evenly distributed throughout the cookie dough.
6. In Zone 1 of the Ninja Dual Zone air fryer, select the BAKE function and preheat it to 180°C in few minutes.
7. Roll the cookie dough into approximately 10 equal-sized balls and place them on a baking sheet that fits in Zone 1 of the air fryer.
8. Place the baking sheet in Zone 1 of the air fryer. Choose BAKE, and set the temperature to 180°C, cooking time to 12 minutes (until the cookies are golden brown around the edges). Press the START/STOP.
9. Once baked, carefully remove the baking sheet from the air fryer and allow the cookies to cool for a few minutes on the sheet before transferring them to a wire rack to cool completely.
10. Once cooled, serve and enjoy the delicious **White Chocolate Cookies**.

PUMPKIN COOKIE WITH CREAM CHEESE FROSTING | SERVES 6

For the cookies:

- 150g plain flour
- 1/2 teaspoon baking powder
- 1/2 teaspoon ground cinnamon
- 1/4 teaspoon ground nutmeg
- 1/4 teaspoon ground ginger
- 1/4 teaspoon salt
- 60g unsalted butter, softened
- 100g light brown sugar
- 100g pumpkin puree
- 1 large egg
- 1/2 teaspoon vanilla extract

For the cream cheese frosting:

- 60g cream cheese, softened
- 30g unsalted butter, softened
- 150g icing sugar
- 1/2 teaspoon vanilla extract.

Prep time: 20 min | Cook time: 12 min

DIRECTIONS

1. In Zone 1 of the Ninja Dual Zone air fryer, select the BAKE function and preheat it to 180°C.
2. In a mixing bowl, whisk together the plain flour, baking powder, ground cinnamon, ground nutmeg, ground ginger, and salt until well combined.
3. In a separate large mixing bowl, cream together the softened butter and light brown sugar until light and fluffy.
4. Add the pumpkin puree, egg, and vanilla extract to the butter mixture. Mix until well incorporated.
5. Gradually add the dry ingredient mixture to the wet mixture, mixing until just combined.
6. Drop spoonfuls of the cookie dough onto a baking sheet or in a baking pan that fits in Zone 1 of the air fryer.
7. Place the baking sheet or pan in Zone 1 of the air fryer.
8. Choose BAKE, and set the temperature to 180°C, cooking time to 12 minutes (until the cookies are set and slightly golden around the edges). Press the START/STOP.
9. Once baked, carefully remove the baking sheet or pan from the Ninja Dual Zone air fryer and allow the cookies to cool completely on a wire rack.
10. While the cookies are cooling, prepare the cream cheese frosting. In a mixing bowl, beat together the softened cream cheese, softened butter, icing sugar, and vanilla extract until smooth and creamy.
11. Once the cookies have cooled, spread or pipe the cream cheese frosting onto each cookie.
12. Serve and enjoy the delicious **Pumpkin Cookies with Cream Cheese Frosting**.

BAKED BRAZILIAN PINEAPPLE | SERVES 4

Prep time: 10 min | Cook time: 12 min

- 1 pineapple
- 2 tablespoons unsalted butter, melted
- 2 tablespoons honey
- 1 teaspoon ground cinnamon
- Juice of 1 lime

DIRECTIONS:

1. In Zone 1 of the Ninja Dual Zone air fryer, select the BAKE function and preheat it to 180°C.
2. Peel and core the pineapple, and cut it into thick slices or wedges.
3. In a small bowl, mix together the melted butter, honey, ground cinnamon, and lime juice.
4. Brush the pineapple slices with the honey-butter mixture, making sure to coat them evenly.
5. Place the pineapple slices in Zone 1 of the air fryer in a single layer.
6. Choose BAKE, and set the temperature to 180°C, cooking time to 12 minutes (until the pineapple is golden brown and caramelized). Press the START/STOP. Turning once halfway through the cooking time.
7. Once baked, carefully remove the pineapple slices from the Ninja Dual Zone air fryer and transfer them to a serving platter.
8. Serve the **Baked Brazilian Pineapple** slices as a delicious dessert or a side dish.

MINI CHEESECAKE | SERVES 2

Prep time: 15 min | Cook time: 15 min

- 150g digestive biscuits
- 50g unsalted butter, melted
- 200g cream cheese
- 60g caster sugar
- 1/2 teaspoon vanilla extract
- 1 egg
- Fresh berries, for garnish (optional)

DIRECTIONS:

1. Crush the digestive biscuits into fine crumbs. This can be done by placing them in a sealable plastic bag and crushing them with a rolling pin or by using a food processor.
2. In a bowl, mix the melted butter with the digestive biscuit crumbs until well combined.
3. Divide the biscuit mixture equally between two small ramekins or oven-safe dishes. Press the mixture down firmly to form the cheesecake crust.
4. In a separate bowl, beat the cream cheese, caster sugar, and vanilla extract until smooth and creamy.
5. Add the egg to the cream cheese mixture and beat until well incorporated.
6. Pour the cream cheese mixture over the prepared biscuit crust in each ramekin, filling them almost to the top. Place the ramekins in Zone 1 of the air fryer, select the BAKE, temperature to 160°C, cooking time to 15 minutes (until the cheesecakes are set and slightly golden around the edges)
7. Once baked, carefully remove the ramekins from the Ninja Dual Zone air fryer and let the mini cheesecakes cool to room temperature.
8. Once cooled, refrigerate the mini cheesecakes for at least 2 hours or until chilled and firm. You can garnish the **mini cheesecakes** with fresh berries, if desired.

APPLE DUTCH BABY | SERVES 4

Prep time: 15 min | Cook time: 20 min

- 2 medium apples, peeled, cored, and sliced
- 2 tablespoons unsalted butter
- 3 large eggs
- 120ml whole milk
- 70g all-purpose flour
- 2 tablespoons granulated sugar
- 1/2 teaspoon vanilla extract
- 1/4 teaspoon ground cinnamon
- Pinch of salt
- Powdered sugar, for dusting
- Maple syrup or honey, for serving

DIRECTIONS:

1. In a skillet or frying pan, melt the butter over medium heat. Add the sliced apples and cook until they are tender and lightly caramelized, about 5 minutes. Set aside.
2. In a mixing bowl, whisk together the eggs, milk, flour, granulated sugar, vanilla extract, ground cinnamon, and salt until smooth and well combined.
3. Grease a round baking dish or oven-safe skillet and pour the batter into it.
4. Arrange the cooked apple slices on top of the batter.
5. Place the baking dish or skillet in Zone 1, Choose BAKE, and set the temperature to 200°C, cooking time to 20 minutes (until the Dutch Baby is puffed up and golden brown). Press the START/STOP.
6. Once cooked, carefully remove the baking dish or skillet from the Ninja Dual Zone air fryer. The Dutch Baby will deflate slightly as it cools.
7. Dust the Apple Dutch Baby with powdered sugar.
8. Serve the **Apple Dutch Baby** warm, cut into wedges, and drizzle with maple syrup or honey.

RICOTTA LEMON POPPY SEED CAKE | SERVES 4

Prep time: 15 min | Cook time: 30 min

- 125g ricotta cheese
- 100g unsalted butter, softened
- 150g granulated sugar
- 2 large eggs
- Zest of 1 lemon
- Juice of 1/2 lemon
- 1 teaspoon vanilla extract
- 150g all-purpose flour
- 1 teaspoon baking powder
- 1 tablespoon poppy seeds
- Pinch of salt
- Icing sugar, for dusting.

DIRECTIONS:

1. In a mixing bowl, combine the ricotta cheese, softened butter, and granulated sugar. Mix until creamy and well combined.
2. Add the eggs, lemon zest, lemon juice, and vanilla extract to the bowl. Mix until smooth.
3. In a separate bowl, whisk together the all-purpose flour, baking powder, poppy seeds, and salt.
4. Gradually add the dry ingredients to the wet ingredients and mix until just combined. Avoid overmixing.
5. Grease a round baking pan that fits in the air fryer basket and pour the cake batter into it.
6. Place the baking pan in Zone 1 of the air fryer, choose BAKE, and set the temperature to 160°C, cooking time to 30 minutes (until a toothpick inserted into the center comes out clean). Press the START/STOP.
7. Once cooked, carefully remove the baking pan from the Ninja Dual Zone air fryer and let the cake cool in the pan for a few minutes.
8. Transfer the cake to a wire rack to cool completely.
9. Dust the **Ricotta Lemon Poppy Seed Cake** with icing sugar before serving.

Printed in Great Britain
by Amazon

24049705R00064